CAPTURING THE SPIRIT OF

Ordinary People, Extraordinary God

HEALED!

—PRESENT DAY STORIES OF—

Divine Healing and How It Happens

ANDY & CATHY SANDERS

5 Fold Media
Visit us at www.5foldmedia.com

"My heart was refreshed and my spirit was stirred as I read *Healed!: Present Day Stories of Healing and How it Happens*, by my dear friends Andy and Cathy Sanders. This is a timely message for the bride of Christ! Each chapter is a journey from pain to victory. I believe that the reader will not only experience God's healing power, but they will also find that they are living at a new level of faith. This book truly captures the supernatural. It's destined to be a classic!"

- **Patrick Schatzline**
Founder of Remnant Ministries International
Author of *Why Is God So Mad at Me?*; *I Am Remnant*;
and *Unqualified: Where You Can Begin to be Great*
www.iamremnant.me

Healed! Present Day Stories of Divine Healing and How It Happens
5 Fold Media ©2015
Published by 5 Fold Media, LLC
www.5foldmedia.com

All rights reserved. No part of this book may be reproduced, stored in a retrieval system, or transmitted in any form or by any means—electronic, mechanical, photocopy, recording, or otherwise—without prior written permission of the copyright owner.

The real life stories in this book have been compiled by Andy Sanders, the founder of 5 Fold Media, who is the exclusive publisher of the *Capturing the Supernatural*™ series. In some cases, names and descriptions of persons mentioned have been changed in order to protect the identity of those who do not wish to be made known publicly. Each contributor has signed a document specifying that every part of their story is true and precise to the best of their knowledge.

Unless otherwise noted, all Scripture quotations are taken from the Holy Bible, New International Version®, NIV® Copyright © 1973, 1978, 1984, 2011 by Biblica, Inc.® Used by permission. All rights reserved worldwide.

Scripture quotations marked "NKJV™" are taken from the New King James Version®. Copyright © 1982 by Thomas Nelson, Inc. Used by permission. All rights reserved.

Scripture quotations marked NLT are taken from the Holy Bible, New Living Translation, copyright 1996, 2004. Used by permission of Tyndale House Publishers, Inc., Wheaton, Illinois 60189. All rights reserved.

Scripture quotations marked AMP are taken from the Amplified® Bible, Copyright © 1954, 1958, 1962, 1964, 1965, 1987 by The Lockman Foundation Used by permission.

ISBN: 978-1-942056-02-7
Library of Congress Control Number: 2015904676

Printed in the USA.

Contents

Introduction ... 7

Physical Healing

The Nurse with the Industrial Fan ... 13
The Supernatural Power of His Presence ... 25
Right Where You Are ... 51
For Freedom's Sake ... 59
Chronic No More ... 71
Out of a Coma ... 81
The Best Mother on Earth ... 91

Emotional Healing

Restoring the Shame ... 101
Making Room for the Supernatural ... 111

Healing Anointing

Prayer in the Cave ... 133
In the Name of Jesus, Get Up! ... 145
Led, Stumbling, into the Plan ... 153
The Simple Miracle of Healing ... 185

You Can Be Healed!

Why Are Some Healed and Others Not? ... 197
Causes of Sickness and Disease ... 207
Remember the Stones ... 221
How to Receive Your Healing ... 225

Conclusion ... 229

INTRODUCTION

The Bible is full of the miraculous—Moses parting the Red Sea, Daniel saved from the lion's den, Elijah calling fire down from heaven, Naaman healed from leprosy, Jesus multiplying the loaves and fishes then healing countless numbers of people, and Peter walking on the water, among many others. The Word of God is a rich resource for proving that God saves and heals. Yet, in spite of all these wonderful stories of faith and miracles, many people live their lives every day without ever seeing any form of divine intervention.

We live in a day and age when our physical bodies, minds, and emotions are constantly battling in an onslaught designed to make us unproductive people. There are sicknesses and diseases that have developed in the last several decades that were never even heard of, let alone diagnosed, fifty years ago. Stress from work and relational issues wears on us, distracting us from our purpose in life. At times, we can become so drained by the day's end that it takes the last reserve of our energy to drag ourselves into bed, just to start over again in the morning.

Is this how God intended for us, His children, to live? I don't think so.

While ministering at a Christian campus recently, my classrooms were filled with hungry young college students from all around the country and of various backgrounds. These were predominantly Christian students who were there to learn and study how to better themselves for Christian service. As I got to know some of the students, I found that not everyone who attended this Christian school believed that miracles truly can happen today. From what I gathered, about a

CAPTURING THE SUPERNATURAL: HEALED!

third to a half of the faculty actually believed, and some taught that miracles don't happen anymore.

I have found that most people who don't believe in miracles quickly change their belief system when they or someone they love are in dire need of divine intervention. It is interesting how many non-believing Christians suddenly believe that God can work miracles when they are in a life-or-death situation. It is in those crucial moments that they cry out for God to help, hoping that He will give them a sign, show the way, or deliver them from their current problem.

Why does this change of heart happen?

> It took a miracle for us to come to salvation to begin with, so it should not be any surprise that miracles continue to work in our lives.

I believe that deep within us, rooted in the day that we were given new life, is the truth that the Spirit of God lives inside of us and that the Spirit living *in* us is capable of incredible, miracle-working power. It took a miracle for us to come to salvation to begin with, so it should not be any surprise that miracles continue to work in our lives. It is no longer God *with* us, as the disciples were with Jesus when He walked on the earth, but now it is God *in* us because He gave us the Holy Spirit to live inside of us every day of our lives once we believed in Jesus.

To them God willed to make known what are the riches of the glory of this mystery among the Gentiles: which is Christ in you, the hope of glory (Colossians 1:27 NKJV).

Jesus Demonstrates the Way

While Jesus was with us on earth, He taught and demonstrated the power of the kingdom over the physical and spiritual world, declaring sicknesses to be healed and commanding the enemy to flee. Up to that moment nobody had ever seen anyone quite like Him.

INTRODUCTION

When Jesus had finished saying these things, the crowds were amazed at his teaching, for he taught with real authority—quite unlike their teachers of religious law (Matthew 7:28-29 NLT).

We know that Jesus did many miracles that were recorded in the Bible. But there were countless more that weren't written down. We know this from what John records in his gospel:

Jesus also did many other things. If they were all written down, I suppose the whole world could not contain the books that would be written (John 21:25 NLT).

But Jesus could not remain with us for eternity. In Jesus' final moments with His disciples, He reassured them that they did not have to be afraid and told them that they would be better off when He was gone, because only then would the Holy Spirit, their Helper, come and live in them.

Nevertheless I tell you the truth. It is to your advantage that I go away; for if I do not go away, the Helper will not come to you; but if I depart, I will send Him to you (John 16:7 NKJV).

Earlier Jesus told us that anyone who believes (that includes you and me) would not only be able to see those same miracles in their own lives but greater. This isn't to say that we have more power than Jesus. It is the simple truth that Jesus was only one person, but He gave *every* believer His power and authority, so it is the exponential power of millions of believers acting in faith and authority that we now possess to see miracles working.

I tell you the truth, anyone who believes in me will do the same works I have done, and even greater works, because I am going to be with the Father (John 14:12 NLT).

Why Do We Doubt?

Most doubt is rooted in fear. Fear that we will be disappointed if things don't go as we hoped, or fear that others will see us as fake or hypocritical if we step out and believe for something and it never comes to pass. Fear of trusting God with something *this big*. Fear is pervasive in our world, and it is this fear and doubt that is holding back the promises of God from our lives.

Capturing the Supernatural: Healed!

Then Jesus said to the disciples, "Have faith in God. I tell you the truth, you can say to this mountain, 'May you be lifted up and thrown into the sea,' and it will happen. But you must really believe it will happen and have no doubt in your heart. I tell you, you can pray for anything, and if you believe that you've received it, it will be yours" (Mark 11:22-24 NLT).

Jesus doesn't lie to us. He wouldn't say these things to us if He didn't mean them! Many times the reason we are not seeing Him work in our lives is not because He is powerless in our situation. Instead it is our lack of faith, our doubting, that limits His power in us. Are we using what He has given us? Do we really believe in our hearts that Jesus can work miracles on our behalf? Jesus repeatedly told His disciples not to doubt, but to simply believe (see Matthew 14:31; 21:21; and Luke 24:38).

Miracles Happen Today

Not only do we know that miracles happen today because the Bible says that they do, we have experienced the miraculous in our own lives. We also have heard testimony after testimony of amazing stories about how God is alive and well, working through the lives of people every day. This book contains just a few of those stories.

What you are about to read are real-life stories from thirteen different people from many different backgrounds and walks of life. Each story is a "snapshot" of a supernatural healing event that occurred in the writer's actual life or through them to heal someone else. Many of these people have experienced several different instances in which they saw and experienced divine healing, either physically or emotionally. Our prayer is that as you read these stories, you will be filled with faith and hope that the same God who was able to work miracles in the lives of those who have shared their stories here is able to work in your life too. As a believer, you have already been given the power and authority to speak to the problems and issues in your life. Can you imagine what would happen if we all just simply believed that it is really true?

If you are not a Christian, don't stop reading now. You are about to read some things that you have never read before—life-changing, documented stories of how ordinary people encounter an extraordinary God!

CAPTURING THE SUPERNATURAL
Ordinary People, Extraordinary God

PHYSICAL HEALING

The Nurse with the Industrial Fan

Andy Sanders

The Nurse with the Industrial Fan

Andy Sanders

It was a beautiful, sunny weekend in the Midwest. Excitement hung in the air as my wife, Cathy, prepared for her graduation in just a few weeks after four long years of Bible college. Little did we know the weekend would quickly turn into a nightmare.

It had been a great day as we planned and prepared for the next few weeks. She was busy studying for final exams and finishing up last details for her classes. This moment was a milestone, and we were eager to see what God had in store for our lives over the next few years as I finished up my training at the same Bible college. We had no idea what was about to transpire in my life. It went from really great to extremely ugly in just a few short hours.

I am not the type of person who gets sick easily. I practically grew up in the gym and loved playing sports. Minus the standard college foods like fried chicken, pizza, soda, sugary desserts, French fries, and greasy cheeseburgers, we were generally in great health. Life was good.

From Bad to Worse

Things began to change that afternoon. Suddenly, I started to feel very strange; something just did not seem right. I felt like my head and upper body were starting to quickly come under a severe sickness for no apparent reason. Normally when I don't feel good I take a nice hot bath, so I filled the tub with hot water and got in. This was very different though. Within just a few minutes I knew something was terribly wrong. I called Cathy into the bathroom and told her how awful I felt. She took my temperature and it was 103.8 degrees! In shock, she took it a few more times and it registered the same. Because we didn't have insurance at the time, we contacted our doctor's office and they suggested that with a fever that high spiking that fast I should get to the emergency room as quickly as possible.

Cathy helped me get dressed and into the car, as I wasn't able to move very quickly by this time. We got to the nearest hospital and they admitted me right away. Because we did not have insurance they informed us that we would have to pay for the cost of the visit. We didn't know much about how hospital visits and billing worked because we had hardly ever needed them. Thinking we would have to pay the bill right then and there, and knowing we didn't have enough money to cover it, we requested a transfer to another hospital that appeared to be more welcoming to college students. We were living in a college town with several secular and Christian universities and colleges close by; one particular hospital had a reputation for helping those in our situation. Most of us back then did not have any insurance once we'd left our hometowns and went to college—especially smaller Bible colleges. We were transferred by ambulance to the other hospital. At that stage the doctors could not yet determine why my fever was so high, even with IVs and medicine pumping through my body.

The new hospital immediately took me upstairs and put me in a room by myself. We had no family there, so Cathy remained with me most of the time, except when she had to leave the room to update family back home. Cell phones were new and we didn't have one yet. Cathy had to use a pay phone to call out of the hospital. A what? Yes, you read that right, a pay phone. These were large phones attached to the wall of the building with a slot to insert change so you could dial your number. Long distance calls were more expensive, asking for more change every few minutes. Or, like most college students did, you could make a collect call; doing this allowed you freedom from a massive amount of quarters because the person receiving the call agreed to pay for it. Thank God for modern technology, right?

The head doctor came in and stated that they needed to work fast to get the 103.8 temperature down to avoid any brain damage. If I hadn't felt so sick at the time I probably would have laughed. If I hadn't had

The Nurse with the Industrial Fan

brain damage by now I probably never would. Growing up I had been hit in the head with a baseball bat, played football with at least one major concussion, took martial arts and was regularly hit in the head through various contact sports, not to mention the stupid moves I had made on a BMX bike, and a few street fights. Right now all I was concerned about was figuring out why my fever had gone from normal to 103.8 degrees in less than an hour.

> Right now all I was concerned about was figuring out why my fever had gone from normal to 103.8 degrees in less than an hour.

They increased the IV solution and gave me heavier pain and fever-reducing medicines. The doctor told us both that if we did not get the fever down soon it could be trouble for my body. By this time I had endured at least two hours of treatments, IVs, doctors poking and prodding me, and still nothing had changed. Every time a nurse or doctor took my temperature it always registered 103.8 degrees.

Because it was a weekend, many of our friends had either gone home for a few days or were catching up on work or studying for exams. This made it tough on my wife. Cathy contacted our local pastor there in town and our families at home and had me placed on multiple prayer chains. In spite of all we had learned about faith and trusting God, I could see panic and frustration in Cathy's eyes as the night wore on with no change, no reason, and no solution for my dangerously high temperature. What was causing it to stay so high and for so long? All this time I was being put through a series of tests to try to figure out what was wrong, but they still came up with no immediate answer.

Another hour dragged by with no change. Now the doctor came in and ordered a spinal tap to check for spinal meningitis. I didn't really like that idea because I don't like needles in general, let alone going into my spine. This was not my idea of a treatment plan. The doctor pulled my wife aside to talk to her privately about the concerns he had about my condition.

While we waited for the call to get the spinal tap, the doctor ordered that I be stripped of my hospital gown, and had ice positioned on my head and various parts of my body. They told my wife to put a cold, wet

Capturing the Supernatural: Healed!

towel on and around my head and to keep rewetting the towel when it got warm. Even after all the ice and the great job my wife did with trying to cool my head down, my body was still too hot. Like anyone with a high temperature, I felt cold on the inside but burning hot on the outside. My temperature did not budge.

Medical Practice?

Eventually they took me for the spinal tap. My mother had once told me that I had had a spinal tap at the age of two, but I didn't remember it at all. If you have ever had a spinal tap, you know what I am about to relate. It was a bit scary, to say the least. As a teaching hospital this facility had the right to let me be used as a guinea pig for medical students in training while under supervision.

Now, let's get something straight here. I am okay with a needle prick in the finger by some medical student, but when I saw a medical student who appeared to be just as nervous and scared as I was getting ready to insert a long and large medical needle into the small space surrounding my spinal cord, I wasn't happy about that all. I spoke up to the leading physician who was supervising the student and he did not feel too concerned, but he wasn't the one being used as a human pincushion by a student with trembling hands! I had to lay there crunched in a ball while the female college student, who looked younger than I was, performed her first spinal tap—on me.

I was relieved when I saw the doctor prepare everything and then insert the needle into my spine. I was thinking, *This isn't so bad*, when, to my surprise, it became apparent that he was just showing her what to do. She took over and then I felt a push in my lower spine. Scared as can be, the young student slowly pushed the needle deeper. I could tell she was shaking as she tried to get the needle to where the doctor's instructions were leading when I felt a burst of pain. She'd hit a nerve! And not just any nerve, *the* nerve, the spinal cord that ran the length of the spine. Yup! That is the one she barely touched. I moved forward in severe pain as the aftershock of something touching that nerve resonated throughout my entire body. When I moved she panicked and let go, causing even more pain. This would have been bad even if I had been

The Nurse with the Industrial Fan

feeling great, but I still had the 103.8 temperature. I'd felt completely miserable before the needle went into my back. Thankfully the doctor stepped in quickly and guided the needle the rest of the way.

Before long, the fluids were collected and the supervising doctor instructed the young student to slowly pull out the needle. The procedure was done! After checking out the insertion point, the doctor said he didn't initially see any visible concerns in my spinal fluid that would suggest severe infection; it was the correct color and normal in appearance. The test would be back in several hours, and in the meantime they would continue to try to get my fever down. They got me back into a normal position on the bed and wheeled me back to my private room where Cathy was waiting and praying.

By then, I could feel the fever starting to take a toll on my body. It had now been over four hours that I'd had this extremely high fever. We were baffled that IVs, medicines, and being stripped down to nothing and practically covered with ice and cold towels had done nothing to decrease my temperature.

While I was having the spinal tap the doctor had asked for the temperature in my room to be turned down as low as possible. I think I recall the nurse saying that it was turned down to sixty-two degrees or something like that. I just remember that it was very cold when I returned. We waited patiently for the test results to come back. I started to feel very weak and the reality that something could be very seriously wrong with my body began to creep into my mind. During this time Cathy prayed over me, quoted Scriptures, and left occasionally to make phone calls on the pay phone to keep family and friends updated on my progress, or lack thereof.

A New Nurse

While Cathy was on the phone I heard the door open and I saw that a nurse I did not recognize came in. She wasn't too tall and had bleached blonde, perfectly curly hair. She looked to be about thirty to thirty-five years old. Her uniform was crisp and well kept. Other than that, nothing else really stood out about her. I didn't think it was strange for a new nurse to come in; I just assumed another shift had started. Somewhat

Capturing the Supernatural: Healed!

dazed now, I remember looking up as she walked to me. She looked me over, checked some information on my chart on a clipboard, and said with a Southern accent, "Yeah. Still trying to get that fever down, right?" I nodded in reply. She touched my foot and said, "We'll get that taken care of for you. I'll be right back."

She left and in a few minutes came back with a heavy duty, industrial yellow fan. I distinctly remembered that type of fan because they used the same kind when I had worked at a Chrysler factory years ago. It was an extremely hot factory with little air flow in my department. It was sometimes over 90 to 100 degrees with severe, windless humidity, and they used the fans to help the workers stay cool while they worked. Those factory fans looked exactly like the one the nurse brought into my room and plugged in. The wind power created from that fan was awesome in that little private hospital room. She told me to stay uncovered and keep cold water on my head while the fan blew on me; that would bring my temperature down. Then the nurse politely left the room and I never saw her again. I remembered thinking, *How in the world did she get that huge fan on the pole in this room so fast?* I also wondered, *How did she move it in here by herself?* Somehow she had done it all alone.

Shortly after she left, Cathy came back into the room and asked about the fan. I told her that a new nurse I had never seen before brought it in for me. With the fan blowing on me and new rounds of cold towels from Cathy, I instantly started feeling better. When I say instant, it was literally like that! My wife left the fan on, no matter how much I complained of feeling cold.

About thirty minutes after the nurse left, the doctor who was handling my care came back into the small room, nearly tripping over the cord and almost knocking the fan over. He looked bewildered as he looked first at the fan and then at me and said, "What's with this fan? What is this fan doing in here? I didn't order this fan to be in here." I told him about the new nurse and how she had brought the fan in. He looked confused and said, "But I didn't order this. What nurse was it?" I described her to the doctor, and he shook his head and said, "I don't remember seeing a nurse like that on the floor tonight. In fact, there isn't a nurse like that in this whole hospital that I am aware of. Where did she

The Nurse with the Industrial Fan

come from? How did she know you were here? And, where did she get this fan?" I told him that she did not tell me where she came from and that I assumed that she was just another nurse in the area.

Then I told the doctor that I was starting to feel much better and asked if he could check my temperature again. He turned off the fan and took my temperature and then checked it again. To both of our surprise, it was almost back down to normal! He prodded and poked around my body, asked me several questions, and then said, "It looks like you might be coming out of this hospital much more quickly than we thought." He ordered a few more tests and turned the fan back on, insisting that it keep blowing on my body with the cold towels just like the nurse had said. Cathy and I were just as puzzled as he was. We were shocked, but our faith began to rise at that moment.

> I described her to the doctor, and he shook his head and said, "I don't remember seeing a nurse like that on the floor tonight. In fact, there isn't a nurse like that in this whole hospital that I am aware of."

After a little while I started to really feel good. I could tell the fever had broken and that I was ready to get clothed again, out of bed, and away from the fan. It became obvious to my wife as well and we began to laugh and joke, knowing that everything was going to be just fine.

The doctor came back into the room soon and said that there wasn't a nurse on duty at the hospital that night who matched the description I had given him. Oddly, he went on to tell us that he hadn't worked with anyone who fit that description that day on his shift. He did say that there was a lady with blonde hair on the floor, but she did not fit the description that I gave. He said he had to rule her out because he knew exactly where she had been at the time. This nurse with the fan was a "mystery" nurse to us all. To add further mystery, they were also not sure where that fan actually came from. The doctor said that he had someone inquire further about the fan and he believed that all the hospital's fans were accounted for and were either in repair or in use at

CAPTURING THE SUPERNATURAL: HEALED!

the time. He said he would check into it again, but I never heard back about the fan issue because I left the hospital not long after that.

When the doctor came back in to check my temperature, it was normal. We were ecstatic! We knew that the hand of God had miraculously intervened. The doctor had me wait a bit longer there to confirm that it would remain stable, which it did. In the meantime he said that I could start preparing to go home. The normal nurse on call for the night came back in and had the IV removed. We were then able to shut the yellow fan off. After that, Cathy got the cold towels off me and before long I was dried off and ready to get my clothes back on. The doctor came in one more time to check my temperature and said, "It's okay for you to go home and get some rest," with a smile on his face. We grabbed our belongings and off we went through the quiet corridors that night, and I walked right out of the hospital. Cathy helped me into our little red car and she drove us both back to our apartment across from the college campus. We didn't waste much time getting into bed. We were exhausted from all the medical drama and it was really late. We turned off our alarms and fell into a deep, restful sleep.

But this story has a second installment with a wholly different kind of rescue.

Quarantined!

I remember waking up to a phone ringing next to our bed, jangling in our ears. That was back in the day when phones had a traditional telephone ring. There were no melodic ringtones, just a harsh ringing. We both woke up. I recall the beautiful sunshine piercing through the blinds and how wonderful it felt to be in bed relaxing after such a rough night. I think it was around 11 o'clock on a Sunday morning. Cathy picked up the phone and it was a nurse at the hospital. The nurse said my spinal tap tested positive for spinal meningitis bacteria and I had to come back into the hospital to be quarantined immediately. She said that this was a precautionary measure required by law because it was so contagious. She asked how I was feeling and Cathy told her that I looked just fine. She asked if I had a slight headache from the spinal tap, but we told her that I wasn't having any problems at all. In spite of how well I felt, she insisted that I come back to the hospital immediately.

The Nurse with the Industrial Fan

When I protested again and told her I really did feel fine, she said if I did not come in they would have to send the police to escort me because of the regulations concerning spinal meningitis. They especially could not risk it because I was connected to a college. So, feeling just fine, we drove back to the hospital and I, unfortunately, checked myself back in.

For a brief time I had been feverless and happy, but not for long. They said I had to be admitted for over a week for treatment! Once I had been installed in the quarantine room and they started hooking me up to an IV and medicines, I developed a blinding headache. Not only did I feel horrible due to pain in my head, but the more medicine they pumped into me, the worse I felt. I was being treated for something that I no longer had; Jesus had healed me! They were forcing me to be treated for something that was already gone and out of my system, and my body was reacting against it. I consistently told them that I was not feeling good because of the treatments, so they treated me with more medication to mask the side effects of the medicines they were giving me for the spinal meningitis that I didn't have. Because I was in a quarantined room, Cathy and any other visitors who came to see me had to wear a face mask and gloves the whole time they were in the room. Nobody was allowed to eat in my room, so Cathy had to leave to eat meals in the waiting area or the cafeteria. She was preparing for her final exams and did her best, trying to study sitting next to me. The whole ordeal affected some of her grades, but a few of her teachers told her that they would drop her final exam grade and average her other grades from the semester; they knew it had been a tough few weeks. It was wonderful to have professors who were kind and compassionate.

After more than a week they were still treating me as if I had spinal meningitis, even though I was showing no further symptoms. Not once did I have a temperature while I was back in the hospital under quarantine. Unfortunately, I was still in quarantine during my wife's college graduation. The hospital staff was kind enough to let me leave the hospital for a few hours in a wheelchair and wearing a face mask to watch Cathy walk across the stage in the ceremony. My father was in town and he wheeled me into the auditorium just before her name was called and right back out afterward. I was excited for her but wished I could have enjoyed the moment with her.

CAPTURING THE SUPERNATURAL: HEALED!

Home at Last

After being in the hospital a long time, I was sent home. I am convinced that I was healed in that little private waiting room once that blonde nurse touched my foot and turned on that fan. I am not a medical doctor by any means, but I believe that when I was brought back in to be quarantined, they were treating me out of precaution. They were treating me for something that no longer existed in my body because the Lord had already healed it. The effects of that type of medicine being put into my body for seven full days could have really been severe. I wasn't feeling sick because I was sick; it was the harsh medicines being pumped into a healthy body that made me feel ill. It is another miracle that I did not suffer anything worse from all the powerful medicines they put into me.

There is no doubt in my mind that God healed me! The mystery nurse was never seen again by me or anyone else who was around us that night. Whether or not she was an angel, it was truly divine that she was there and more than likely saved my life. My second miracle was recovering from this with no adverse effects.

Andy Sanders was divinely healed from a life-threatening blood disorder at two years of age. Three weeks before his high school graduation, he died of a drug overdose and, after an encounter with God, came back to life. God supernaturally set him free from drugs and alcohol. Andy earned his doctorate in Christian education at Freedom Seminary in Rogers, Arkansas. He has been preaching since 1993 and served as pastor and on staff. Andy is a former writer for venues such as the Elijah List, Identity Network, and Where Eagles Gather (a combined audience of over 350,000). After traveling in ministry extensively for four years, the Sanders founded 5 Fold Media. Andy and his wife, Cathy, travel and minister and have two children. Find out more about Andy at www.andycathysanders.com.

HEALED!

The Supernatural Power of His Presence

Gregory Bogart

The Supernatural Power of His Presence

Gregory Bogart

It started with an intermittent sharp pain in my left ear, left side of my throat, and the left side of my tongue. At first the frequency of occurrence and the intensity of pain were minimal, but they increased over time. About August of 2009 I began to notice that my ability to enunciate words was becoming slightly hindered as well as my ability to manipulate food while chewing. I scheduled an appointment with my primary physician to investigate the cause of the pain and my speech impediment. During the examination I was asked to stick out my tongue. The look on my doctor's face showed concern. He asked, "How long has your tongue been drooping to one side?" I answered, "I haven't noticed my tongue drooping to one side." He lifted a mirror to my face and I stuck out my tongue. Sure enough, my tongue was drooping to the left. He asked me to move my tongue to a center position and I could not. It was now apparent to me that I had lost some of my ability to control the movement of my tongue. What was going on? My primary physician set up an appointment with an ear, nose, and throat doctor for a specialized examination of my symptoms.

Approximately one month later I was being examined by the specialist who I will call Dr. N. He conducted a thorough examination of my ears, nose, throat, and tongue. His initial diagnosis was inconclusive. He was unable to ascertain the source of my symptoms. I was puzzled. The pain had increased both in frequency and intensity to the point where it was becoming increasingly difficult to perform my daily responsibilities. The pain jarred me constantly and I could not eat or speak well. I had been certain he would discover the reason for these conditions. Dr. N. recommended that I see a neurologist thinking there might be a neurological source for my symptoms. I readily agreed. Dr. N arranged an appointment with a local neurologist whom I will designate as Dr. G. However it would be almost another month before my appointment with him.

The Diagnosis

Dr. G.'s diagnosis was glossopharyngeal neuralgia, a condition in which there are repeated episodes of severe pain in the ear, nose, throat, tonsils, and tongue. It is believed to be caused by irritation of the ninth cranial nerve, called the glossopharyngeal nerve. Possible sources of the irritation are blood vessels pressing on the glossopharyngeal nerve, growths at the base of the skull that are pressing on the nerve, or tumors or infections of the throat and mouth pressing on the nerve. In some cases, the source of the irritation is never found. I had the pain associated with this condition in three of the five target areas; however, Dr. G. was unable to discover with certainty the source of the pain. He referred me to the neurological department of Strong's Memorial Hospital in Rochester, New York for a second opinion of his diagnosis. Again it would be another month before I would be seen by the next round of experts. It seemed to me that they were not treating this with the urgency it deserved.

The examination at Strong's Memorial Hospital proved to be both disconcerting and frustrating. Disconcerting because the attending doctor discovered a significant lump in my tongue and frustrating because I could not understand how these other doctors had missed the lump. I had been running from one specialist to another for months only to discover a lump in my tongue that seemed so very easily discovered by the examining doctor at Strong's Memorial. He suggested I return to Dr. N., my ear, nose, and throat specialist to have a biopsy conducted at once. Dr. N. scheduled me immediately, conducted the biopsy, and sent it to the lab for analysis. He sent me home with the expectation

The Supernatural Power of His Presence

of receiving a call from him within twenty-four hours with the lab's findings.

Waiting to find out if I had cancer was a surreal experience for my wife and me. I had been as healthy as the proverbial horse throughout my life. I had not smoked cigarettes for many years and did not drink. Sickness was something that we rarely dealt with, with the exception of the occasional cold or minor stomach bug. But now we were faced with the possibility that I might have cancer, the "Big C." An agreement, unstated but understood, seemed to exist between us as we spent the day avoiding any conversation about me having cancer. It seemed as though we were silently reassuring ourselves and each other that it would be benign. After all, I was a pastor of a local church. God had called me to preach the gospel and to teach and disciple those whom He had put in my care. My ability to speak was essential to the call of God on my life; surely this was simply a test of our faith. We leaned into our love for one another, exercising our faith in the goodness of God, believing that the lump in my tongue would be benign.

My cell phone rang at around 7 o'clock that evening. I thought nothing of it. A pastor's phone rings frequently. I looked at the number on the call display—it was Dr. N.'s number. The moment was here when God would prove His faithfulness once again. "Hello!" I answered it.

"Yes, is this Greg?" asked Dr. N.

"Yes, sir, it is," I replied.

"Greg, I'm afraid I have some bad news. The tumor is malignant. I'm very sorry!"

I remember that moment well. It was as if time stopped. I had just heard what I had believed all day I would never hear. I suddenly realized that everyone I loved and who loved me—my family, my church family, my friends—everyone was about to be affected by the fact that cancer was in my body. I do not remember being afraid, but felt strangely unaffected emotionally. It was as if my soul had been suspended and my spirit man took over. A surreal calmness was present—the peace of

Capturing the Supernatural: Healed!

> I suddenly realized that everyone I loved and who loved me—my family, my church family, my friends—everyone was about to be affected by the fact that cancer was in my body.

God that passes understanding maybe? I replied matter-of-factly, "OK, doctor, what do we do now?" As I reflect back on that moment I realize that the spirit of faith which God had cultivated in me for years was in control; therefore peace was present. God's faithfulness was already manifesting to lead me and all those affected by this attack to a place of victory.

First Steps of the Journey

Dr. N. outlined the process and presented me with a number of options for moving forward. The most important one was choosing the cancer facility at which I would prefer treatment. I gave him my choice based on proximity to my home. He said he would schedule an immediate appointment for me, and with that he ended our conversation. Thus begins my testimony of the faithfulness of my Father in heaven, which leads to the most profound supernatural encounter with the manifest presence of Jesus that I have ever experienced.

My wife and I arrived at the cancer institute near the middle of November 2009. I was scheduled to undergo a battery of tests and examinations over a three-day period. The drive had been three and a half hours through early morning darkness and the uncertainty of what lay ahead. The only certainty was that the enemy of cancer had to be defeated. When we entered the facility we were struck by the number of people who were already there. The lobby was full of people just like us—some just beginning the process, others well into their battle and recovery. The patients who were well into the battle were easily identifiable by the hats and scarves covering heads that had lost their hair. The effects of fatigue from chemotherapy and radiation, which I would come to know well, could be seen on the countenances of many. I noticed that all patients were attended by someone—a family member, a friend, or a health care worker. I was no exception. My best friend and most precious family member, my wife, Debra, was by my side. Her strength and selfless love were and still are a constant source of comfort and strength to me. My Father is right—a virtuous wife is a crown to her husband and a good thing to find!

After completing the initial registration process, we proceeded to the third floor to the head and neck treatment department. I was not prepared for what I was about to see. We checked in and found seats in a crowded waiting room. I began to look about the room, discreetly glancing at the patients. There were several patients with such visible effects of their battle that my faith was challenged to the core on that initial visit. I later discovered that Deb was experiencing the same thing. It was apparent that some had lost their larynx and could only speak by placing a microphone-like device up to their throats, their voices sounding like raspy robots. Others had tubes protruding from their throats that enabled them to breathe. Still others had been disfigured from surgery, some severely. Several had whole sections of their jaw or neck, or both, missing. Satan wasted no time in challenging us about what we observed, insinuating that one of these conditions would be mine to endure. The tempter always draws one's attention to the worst possible outcome in order to engender fear. However, we took solace in the fact that many of the patients who checked in during our long wait had none of these unfortunate and unsightly conditions. Finally, after a long wait the door opened and a nurse called my name. We were both anxious to get on with it. Waiting is not something that a person diagnosed with cancer wants to do. But patience, as we would learn, is an invaluable virtue in the battle with this insidious disease.

Dr. H. walked into the room and greeted me formally, calling me Reverend Bogart, as he introduced himself to us. Dr. H. would be the lead doctor in a team of specialists who would be working to examine and evaluate my case to prescribe a treatment plan with the maximum chance for the best possible outcome. Of course Deb and I believed for the best possible outcome as well, which, for us, was a supernatural healing by God. But doctors often leave God out of the equation. It was at this first visit to Dr. H.'s office that I began to undergo a series

Capturing the Supernatural: Healed!

of necessary indignities in order to fully evaluate the extent of the malignant invasion of my body. The images from the MRI and CAT scan revealed a rather large growth in my tongue. The major factor to be determined was the direction of the growth of the tumor. If it had originated in the front of my tongue and progressed toward the base of my tongue located in the upper throat, the possibility of the cancer spreading from the tongue into my throat or other areas of my neck would be greatly increased. It was the first order of business to discern this direction, and Dr. H. proceeded with all haste.

Nemesis in Sight

He began by having an assistant insert a small camera fixed to the end of a long but narrow probe into one of my nostrils. At the point where the nostril constricts in diameter, slight force is exerted to push the camera beyond that point. It is here that the procedure becomes uncomfortable. Once the camera head is past the constricted point, it enters into the throat area where the base of the tongue is located. The camera must be maneuvered by the assistant to examine the tumor from various angles as well as to thoroughly examine the throat and larynx for any sign of cancer. Whenever the device touched the wall of my throat, it caused an irritating itch producing the overwhelming desire to sneeze—something I could not do. It was a very difficult sensation to overcome. When it was time to examine my larynx, the assistant maneuvered the camera into position and instructed me to pronounce the letter "E" and to hold it until I was told to stop. This produced the same itch but with increased intensity. I would be examined this way many times. I can tell you that some assistants can perform this procedure more skillfully than others.

The doctors, Deb, and I could see the images from the camera on a screen in the room in real time. Dr. H. pointed out the tumor and the scope of its size. There it was in plain sight, my nemesis, my opponent. It had begun with a single rebellious cell spreading its rebellion to other cells, eventually forming a collective mass revolt against the health and wellbeing of my entire body. There it was—the source of my pain, my speech impediment, and by this time, my inability to chew and swallow

The Supernatural Power of His Presence

solid food. I could only drink liquids. This group of mutinous cells had the potential to kill, steal, and destroy my life and the destiny for which God created me if it was not overcome and vanquished from my body.

After the probe was retracted, Dr. H. told us he needed to physically examine the tumor. He would do this by inserting a rather large finger (Dr. H. was a very large man) down my throat to feel the hardness of the tumor near the base of my tongue. I knew this was not going to be pleasant; I possess a highly sensitive gag reflex. Before I could mentally prepare myself, Dr. H. grabbed the back of my head with one hand to prevent me from recoiling from his finger on its way down my throat with force and swiftness. Immediately I began to gag. I could feel my face flush as my whole body went tense. My eyes filled and tears began to run down my face. I fought hard to repel the desire to gag, but could not. Dr. H. pushed down with considerable force on the tumor causing me intense pain while searching out its perimeter to determine the direction of its growth. Deb observed the whole ordeal with a look of uncomfortable disbelief. It was awful! But it was an indignity I would suffer often at the skillful hands of Dr. H. When the good doctor withdrew his finger from my throat, it took me a few minutes to recover. Two procedures and I was done. My mind was shouting, "No more, no more!" What could he possibly do to me next? I laugh when I think back on it now, but it was not funny that first time.

> Before I could mentally prepare myself, Dr. H. grabbed the back of my head with one hand to prevent me from recoiling from his finger on its way down my throat with force and swiftness.

I came to appreciate Dr. H. as a highly skilled and successful head and neck specialist. He was at the top of his field, one of the best head/neck cancer doctors in the country. He was a consummate professional, courteous, but always businesslike. One day as I was sitting in the waiting room awaiting the pleasure of another of Dr. H.'s finger probes, I realized why he carried out his practice in the manner that he did. Every day Dr. H. did battle with the demon of cancer and its affliction upon

Capturing the Supernatural: Healed!

the bodies of very real people. Every day he poked and prodded patients while performing procedures that he knew full well were unpleasant and difficult for them to endure. I realized that the disfigurement of many of those I encountered in his waiting room had been made that way by his scalpel. After surgery he was the one who looked them in the eye, knowing he had done what was necessary and they would bear the mark of it forever. I came to believe that Dr. H. conducted his practice with a professional and businesslike demeanor to remain as emotionally unattached to his patients as possible, and yet with a sufficient measure of respect, compassion, and courtesy. I thank God for the tremendous grace and ability that God has given Dr. H. to help countless thousands fight their battle with cancer. I thank God that he was my lead doctor.

Thankfully there was only one more procedure necessary to determine the direction of the growth of the tumor in my tongue. It was an endoscope. However, for this procedure I would be anesthetized. Hallelujah! Poke me, prod me, do whatever you need to do, just let me be asleep! It was scheduled for the next day. The endoscope was performed and the results analyzed. The tumor had grown in the favorable scenario. This good report washed over us in a wave of hope like a booster shot to our faith. This was the first welcome news in a long time.

Life is Dramatically Changed

While all of these doctor appointments and examinations, tests, and procedures were taking place, my ability to chew and swallow food was diminishing. By November of 2009 I had lost all ability to eat solid food. I could only ingest liquids. The tumor had grown so large that it inhibited my ability to control the movement of my tongue. I was not aware of the role the tongue plays in our ability to chew and swallow solid food. Chewing and swallowing are abilities I had taken for granted. By the time I met Dr. H., I had been unable to take in solid food for two weeks. I was subsisting on vitamin water and juices. Hunger was now another aspect to the battle I was fighting, and it was a constant enemy. Dr. H. suggested that a feeding tube be implanted through my stomach wall through which I could receive nutrients. He said I would

The Supernatural Power of His Presence

be contacted with a specific date and time for the procedure. Deb and I returned home. The call came informing me that the installation of the feeding tube had been scheduled for the end of November. I was not happy that I would have to fight hunger for two more weeks.

By this time the physical and emotional aspects of the battle were beginning to take a toll on me and my wife. Deb found it difficult to cook meals because filling the house with the smell of food only exacerbated my hunger. She felt guilty about eating because I couldn't. Speaking was difficult for me so our conversations became limited. Physical intimacy was not even on the radar. The cancer was slowly stealing the way we lived our lives—stealing from us things that we so took for granted and underappreciated until they were gone. My health and the quality of our life were deteriorating daily. We were trying to maintain our faith, but the situation seemed to be getting worse by the day. God knew our faith needed a boost, and He is always on time.

The Lord Will Preserve

A local pastor friend of mine came to the house during this time. He brought a minister friend of his who was visiting from Uganda. We sat in our living room and I related my situation as best I could. The brother from Uganda listened carefully, and when I finished he asked me a question in his Ugandan accent, "Brother Greg, do you have a prophetic word spoken over your life?"

"Yes," I replied.

Then he quoted Hosea 12:13 to me, "By a prophet the Lord brought Israel out of Egypt, and by a prophet he was preserved" (NKJV). He instructed me to take the prophetic word and read it holding it before the Lord, for it would preserve me through this battle. I received this as being from the Lord. They both prayed for us and left after a refreshing time of fellowship. We were both reminded of the true nature of this attack: to steal the prophetic destiny on our lives. The Devil was not only trying to steal from us but he was attempting to steal God's will for our lives.

Capturing the Supernatural: Healed!

Certainly God would not allow that. Deb and I were both encouraged and strengthened by the visit of these two heavenly messengers.

Battle Plan

The following week we returned to the cancer institute for a consultation with an oncologist to evaluate the results of all the tests and to prescribe a treatment plan. We sat silently waiting for the oncologist to enter the room, trying not to let our imaginations run roughshod over the situation. The oncologist came in and greeted us taking a seat in front of us. He began to summarize my case by saying, "Well, Mr. Bogart, you definitely have cancer."

Deb suddenly interrupted, "What stage is it, doctor?"

He attempted to deflect the question by stating that the stage was basically irrelevant and we needed to focus on the treatment plan. But Deb insisted. He reluctantly answered, "Well, if you must know, it is at stage four. It has spread into the lymph nodes in the left side of your neck."

Neither of us was ready to hear the number four. I fully expected to hear one or two at the most. Tongue cancer is very dangerous because of the fact that it can spread into the lymph nodes, which is life threatening, and that is exactly what had happened. In our minds that translated as the worst possible scenario. In an attempt to push that information away, I asked, "So what is the treatment plan?" The doctor then laid out the plan. We would begin with a series of radiation and chemotherapy treatments. If those did not work, I would have to have surgery. The word *surgery* conjured up images of all the disfigured patients I saw every time I entered Dr. H.'s waiting room, but worst of all was the thought of a glossectomy.

My mind drifted back to the completion of my initial examination by Dr. H.; he had informed me that if the eventual prescribed treatment plan did not work, a glossectomy, which is a partial or complete removal of the tongue, would be necessary in order to save my life. My mind immediately rejected that possibility, though it truly was a possibility. That simply could not happen. My purpose in life is to declare the Word of God. How could I do that without my tongue? No, that would not happen. God was not going to allow that. Every time I was seen by Dr. H., he reminded me of this possibility if the treatment did not work. And every time he did, I had absolutely refused to accept that outcome.

"Mr. Bogart, are you all right?" The oncologist's question snapped me back to my awareness of the present.

"Yes, I'm all right, doctor," I answered. The treatment plan called for eight rounds of chemotherapy and thirty-five rounds of radiation, the most rounds prescribed. The radiation would be administered Monday through Friday over a seven-week period. The chemo would also be administered once a week over that same period of time with the first chemo treatment occurring the week before radiation began. He told me that it was critical that I complete this plan with little or no interruption in the schedule. The treatment would have a better chance of being successful if all treatments were finished within the seven-week time frame. I was determined to complete this regimen on time as it was the best chance to avoid a glossectomy. The major obstacle to a timely completion would be the three-and-a-half-hour drive to the center to undergo the treatments. It was just not feasible. After consulting with Dr. H. and weighing all the options, we decided to have the treatments at University Hospital in Syracuse, New York, which was a little over an hour away from my home. Dr. H. knew an excellent radiologist at University Hospital, who I will call Dr. K., and made all the arrangements for me to see him immediately.

Dr. K. greeted me with a friendly smile and warm demeanor. He had examined all the imaging sent to him by Dr. H. and asked me to tell him the story of how I had ended up in his office. I told him that Dr. H. had repeatedly reminded me of the need for a glossectomy if the prescribed regimen was not successful. At the end of the examination, he informed me that based on his experience he believed the radiation treatments would be successful and surgery would not be necessary. I was greatly

CAPTURING THE SUPERNATURAL: HEALED!

relieved. As we were walking down the hallway toward the reception area, he introduced me to one of his assistants who would actually administer the radiation. I will never forget his words as he introduced me to her! "This is Mr. Bogart. He will be receiving treatment here. Mr. Bogart is a pastor. We must get him back to preaching the good news as soon as possible." My heart filled with faith and joy as I heard those determined words. I was persuaded that God had provided Dr. K. as my radiologist. I cried tears of joy and thanksgiving on the drive home. I couldn't wait to tell Deb the good news. Little did I know in that moment of refreshing joy that the rollercoaster ride of emotional events we were on was about to hit another low.

Hunger Pains

The day arrived to receive my feeding tube. Finally I would be able to satisfy the intense gnawing hunger I had been fighting for a month now. I had been losing a significant amount of weight and was now thinner than at any time in my life. I was absolutely sick of drinking liquids to keep from dehydrating. They all seemed to taste the same and none of them could satisfy my hunger. I needed nutrients, especially protein. But mostly I needed to feel full. I did not realize it, but I had been slowly starving to death surrounded by food I could not eat. Hunger is an insidious way to die. In a desperate attempt to stay alive, your body eats itself to death. I went from 222 pounds to 156 pounds in a month and ten days—66 pounds lost in 40 days. My body was greatly fatigued, and I had lost much physical strength. Physical activity was exhausting, and even thinking could be tiring. I knew that Deb was going to be relieved to know that I would be able to receive nutrition. She had been watching me waste away before her eyes and there was nothing she could do about it. Deb is a good cook, but cooking was something she had done little of in deference to me over the past two months. But today this problem was coming to an end.

> In a desperate attempt to stay alive, your body eats itself to death. I went from 222 pounds to 156 pounds in a month and ten days— 66 pounds lost in 40 days.

The Supernatural Power of His Presence

We arrived at the cancer institute for the appointment we had made previously with Dr. H. to receive my feeding tube implant. As always we checked in at the registration desk. I handed the receptionist my registration card and informed her that we were here for outpatient surgery. She took the card and entered the information into her computer. She looked up at me and said, "I'm sorry, Mr. Bogart, but I do not see that you are scheduled for any surgery today. All I see is an appointment with Dr. H."

Frantically I responded, "There must be a mistake. I am scheduled for a feeding tube implant today. This was the day I am to have the tube put in. Someone called me from here and gave me this date." Her compassionate reply did nothing to remove the anxiety that overwhelmed both of us at that moment. All we could do now was wait to discuss the issue with Dr. H.

When Dr. H. entered the room, greeting me as he always did, he asked how I was. "Not good, doctor," I replied.

"Why? What is wrong, Reverend Bogart?" he asked. Deb informed him of the situation, and he had an assistant investigate the problem immediately. After a while the assistant returned to tell us that my appointment was scheduled for December 10, another ten days away. Whoever had called had given me the wrong date. My heart sank. How could I endure another ten days of hunger? The disappointment was overwhelming.

Dr. H. apologized for the mix-up. He even gave me the option of having the tube installed in his office, but without anesthesia. He finished by saying, "It will be painful, but I will do it if you want." I seriously thought about letting him do it, but, amazingly, in the end I decided to wait until the new date. The thought of another ten days of dealing with hunger did not overcome my aversion to letting the good doctor cut a hole into my stomach through which he could insert the feeding tube the old fashioned way—with a shot of whiskey and a stick to bite down on. As you can imagine, the long drive home was very quiet. Neither of us wanted to verbalize the question we were silently asking: "God, why does this have to be so difficult? How many times can we keep saying to one another, 'Honey, it will be all right. We'll get through this.'"

Capturing the Supernatural: Healed!

The Mask

A few days later I was back at the radiology department at Syracuse University Hospital being fitted for a mask to be worn for the radiation process. Radiation delivery is a very precise procedure. The radiation must be delivered to the target area only to ensure maximum efficiency and to protect the good cells around the target area. Therefore my head would have to remain immobile during treatments. This is the function of the mask. The mask is made of a hard plastic perforated with diamond-shaped holes. The plastic is warmed to be rendered pliable. It is then placed over the face while the patient is lying on their back. The plastic was pressed onto my face, conforming it to the contours of my face. Once this was achieved, it was removed and allowed to cool and harden. When sufficiently hardened, the assistant placed it over my face, making sure it fit snugly but comfortably. Then the mask was secured to the radiation table, ensuring that my head would remain immobile throughout the twenty-minute treatment.

Radiation delivery is computer controlled. Once the mask was deemed suitable and fastened securely to the table, Dr. K. came into the room and marked the mask with a little "X" in several different locations. Light rays from the delivery aperture controlled by the computer shone onto the mask according to predetermined calculations made by Dr. K.; these calculations were based on the magnetic imaging he had previously conducted. These specific spots were where Dr. K. placed the Xs. These markers would assure that my head was properly aligned before each dose of radiation was delivered. It is paramount that each treatment destroys as many cancer cells as possible for the treatment to be a success. After the mask was prepared, I was briefed on the entire procedure from start to finish and sent home.

Shortly thereafter Deb and I returned to the cancer institute to have the feeding tube installed. We met with a nutritionist who calculated the number of calories I would require daily to return to normal weight based on my height. I would need to take six cartons of nutritional energy drinks a day at 360 calories per carton to maintain my weight with minimal exercise. When I first began taking it, I had to proceed at a slow pace to allow my stomach to stretch for it had shrunk significantly.

The Supernatural Power of His Presence

I wanted to just pour the boost in to quickly satisfy the hunger cravings. Within short order the daily requirements of vitamins, minerals, and protein were working to restore my body to health. It was wonderful to feel full again!

An Unexpected Setback

On December 22, 2009, I had my first chemotherapy treatment. It was a four-hour process. After the initial chemo infusion, I was given a specific medicine to counteract the nausea induced by the treatment with instructions on when to take it. The next day I began feeling severely nauseated. Had I taken the medicine incorrectly? Deb called the infusion center and spoke with a nurse who suggested I go to the emergency room at our local hospital. *What now?* I wondered as we drove to the hospital. Was this another setback, a disappointing delay to process and overcome, or was it something easily remedied? I was scheduled to begin radiation treatment the following Monday and needed to be well for that to happen.

The ER doctor began his examination with the usual foray of questions. He ordered a blood test; the blood was drawn and sent to the lab for immediate analysis. An IV was started and I was given medicine to mitigate the severe nausea. The doctor left to care for other patients. After a lengthy time, he returned stating the lab test had come back. He asked me if I was experiencing any pain in my abdominal area. I told him no, and he asked if I was sure. Again I said no. He looked puzzled as he explained that the blood test indicated a highly elevated enzyme level in my pancreas. A normal level is 300, and my level was well over 3,000! He pushed on my abdomen with his fingers, asking me if it hurt. Once again my answer was no. He explained the high level of enzymes was an indication of severe inflammation of the pancreas. The one thing that puzzled him was that I should have been experiencing pain equivalent to a woman in labor if in fact it was pancreatitis. I was admitted and observed for three days, and I was extremely sick!

The doctors at the local hospital seemed baffled by my condition but did nothing to improve it. I was unable to keep any food in my system. Of course the doctors were concerned because I had cancer and knew I had to get well before my treatments could continue. On the third day Deb and

Capturing the Supernatural: Healed!

I were becoming increasingly frustrated with the lack of answers from the attending physician. The nurse on duty that day overheard my wife voicing her concern and suggested that I be transferred to the cancer department at University Hospital in Syracuse, New York. The nurse informed us that the doctor who would most likely agree to a transfer would not be back on duty for three days. My wife was not going to wait another three days. She immediately called the cancer department at University Hospital and talked with a doctor there. She related my situation and he agreed to help us. He spoke with the head of the cancer department and secured a bed for me. Transfer arrangements were made that night and I was transported by ambulance to University Hospital.

The cancer department was a brand-new wing. It was like the Taj Mahal compared to where I had been. I had a private room that was pleasantly decorated, a big screen TV, and a bath with a walk-in shower. The staff members were professional, personable, and very compassionate. Shortly after arriving, the head of the cancer department at University Hospital (who I will refer to as Dr. P.) came in and did a preliminary examination, ordering all the necessary tests. He came back the next morning with a diagnosis. It was, in fact, pancreatitis. He was astonished that I was not experiencing severe pain. However, there was no other explanation for the elevated enzyme level in my pancreas. He prescribed the course of treatment for pancreatitis and said I should see a marked improvement within a few days. Another unknown scare had been diverted. Deb and I were greatly relieved. After a few days I was given a nutritional energy drink at a slow rate through the IV to see if I could keep it down. After one week they deemed me well enough to have my first radiation treatment, as I was already right there. I readily agreed; I was anxious to get on with it. It would be ten days before my enzyme count fell within acceptable levels and I returned home. God in His great mercy supernaturally spared me the severe pain associated with pancreatitis.

Now it was time to start the weekly regimen of chemo and radiation treatments. The drive south to Syracuse along the eastern shore of Lake Ontario is through a stretch of Interstate 81 known as the Snow Belt. Lake effect snow off Lake Ontario can dump several feet of snow in a short amount of time. It is a treacherous drive if lake effect conditions occur. My treatments were taking place during January and February of that year in the dead of winter. But I had to go every day Monday through Friday for seven weeks regardless of the weather. We kept a close eye on weather reports to make necessary arrangements to stay overnight if the weather was threatening. Deb went down with me every Monday to help me through the long day of both radiation and chemo treatments. Tuesday through Friday my youngest son, Joshua, who was twenty at the time, drove me down for my early morning radiation treatments.

Positioned for Treatment

For each treatment, I would announce my arrival at the reception desk and take a seat. Rarely did I have to wait long. I would go in and sit on the radiation table with my feet on the floor. I would swing my right leg up and onto the table followed by my left one, and then lie prone on the table on my back. The assistants would place the mask over my face and secure it to the table, making certain my head was properly aligned. They always asked if I was comfortable, reminding me that if at any time I became stressed just say so and they would immediately stop the treatment and come to my aid. Then they would leave from the room and begin the process.

The radiation machine would engage and slide me backward until my head was centered under a circular aperture. Then I would wait for a minute or so until the machine began to wind up. At a certain point a band in the center of the circular aperture would move in a counterclockwise direction and remain spinning for a good while. It would stop and then resume after a short time and remain spinning until the end of the treatment. The machine would then return me to the original starting point and the assistants would come in, release me from the mask, and I would go home.

Side Effects

After two weeks the side effects of the radiation treatments began to take effect. One particularly egregious effect of radiation is mucus

Capturing the Supernatural: Healed!

buildup in the throat. The amount of buildup varies from individual to individual. And of course I qualified for the severe category! The mucus is very thick and viscous. For these reasons it is very difficult to clear from the throat. I would often choke and begin to gag as I attempted to clear my throat. Many times I vomited what little contents there were in my stomach. Because my buildup was severe I had difficulty sleeping at night, waking often with a choking sensation because of the mucus buildup. As a result I became very fatigued. I slept on the couch in the living room so as not to keep Deb awake at night. I often sat for hours alone at night, desperately wanting to sleep for more than ten minutes at a time. I listened to worship music and whispered prayers to the Lord for His mercy and strength to carry us through to the end. If this was the effect after only two weeks, what would I be like by the end?

> I often sat for hours alone at night, desperately wanting to sleep for more than ten minutes at a time.

Another side effect from treatment was that the mouth, tongue, and throat becomes severely irritated, tender, and painfully sensitive to any contact. At one point I spent three weeks unable to speak at all; even speaking was too painful. Deb bought me a small chalkboard through which I would communicate. Imagine the pain of simply trying to clear my throat of the mucus buildup. It was extremely excruciating, but could not be avoided. And imagine doing that a hundred times a day! I had pain medicine, but it did little to alleviate the pain.

I remember one night feeling very despondent—wondering how much more I could endure with several weeks of treatment yet remaining. In a merciful attempt to comfort me, the Holy Spirit reminded me of the brother from Uganda's instruction. I took the paper on which I had written the prophetic word, and because I could not read it aloud I simply held it over my head so God could see it. There I sat in my miserable condition with God's word to me suspended between me and Him. I was trying hard to believe that there was a necessity within the wisdom of my heavenly Father's will for the measure of my suffering. The Father's word of destiny spoken to me by His prophet stated that

The Supernatural Power of His Presence

He had given me a voice of influence through which He would speak to change the lives of many. I had to overcome by His grace. I could not lose my voice to cancer. In that moment I made a decision. No one was going to remove my tongue. If the treatments did not work then I would throw myself into God's hand and trust in His Word and His power to heal. If I could not do His will here, then I would go home to be with Him. I was resolute in my spirit. The next morning I told my wife of the decision I made and how I arrived at it. I asked her to promise me that if I became incapacitated and could not answer for myself that she would not allow any surgery be performed on my tongue—especially a complete glossectomy. Reluctantly she promised. She was brave to do so! I also told my son that if there was any morning that I refused to go to treatment because of the fatigue, to pick me up and carry me out to the car and take me to treatment. He agreed. He too was very brave!

One night Josh sat up into the night with me to keep me company. At that time Josh was not serving the Lord. He was sitting in the recliner and I was lying on the couch, listening to worship music. Josh got up and came over to me, put his head on my chest, and wept. Through the tears I heard him whisper, "Dad, what kind of man are you? How can you do this?"

I said, "Josh, I trust the Lord to get me through this. You can too." I remember praying in that moment and asking the Father to bring my prodigal son home. Then suddenly, in a small but very discernable measure, I understood my Savior's willingness to undergo horrendous suffering that I might be saved. He endured the indignities and pain of the cross with joy, knowing that many sons would be brought into glory. I heard myself saying to the Lord, "If You use my suffering to bring my son back to You, then the suffering will have been worth every ounce of it." I loved my son so much that I was willing to endure any amount of suffering that he might be saved. It was a powerful revelation but nothing like the one I would experience in the very near future.

The Battle Rages On

Another side effect that plagued me was burnt skin all around my throat area and the sides of my neck. Radiation burns the skin. Imagine

Capturing the Supernatural: Healed!

being sunburned and then continuing to go out and lie in the direct sun day after day. Your burned skin could not heal, and neither could mine. Day after day the same area was exposed to the invisible fire of radiation. After several weeks the skin on the sides of my neck and throat was severely burned and painful to any contact. I was given a special ointment to apply to the burnt areas, which was a delicate process in itself. The slightest touch caused extreme discomfort. I was extremely fatigued due to insufficient sleep, unable to speak or swallow, burnt to a crisp all around my throat, with every cell in my mouth and throat area screaming from the intense pain from clearing my throat of mucus buildup many, many times day and night. I had lost so much weight that when I stood in front of the mirror it was difficult to look at myself. I was skin and bones. This was the state I was in after months under siege from cancer and four weeks of radiation treatments. Quite frankly, I was a pitiful sight. But I was determined to battle on!

Josh and I arrived for another radiation treatment. I had no idea which day it was. After a while you lose track of time. It is just another pain-filled day, just another treatment. The assistants were always so kind, patient, and encouraging. They would always commend me for keeping on track with treatments despite how difficult it was for me. They would escort me into the treatment room and busy themselves with the preparations while I cleared my throat of mucus buildup. I often wondered if they busied themselves to focus on something other than the gross process of me clearing my throat. But I had to clear my throat before getting on that table. It had become very difficult to get through the full twenty-minute treatment without feeling the need to clear my throat at some point. Usually it would be well before the session was over. Sometimes I would have to fight hard not to panic and call out for them to stop for fear I would choke. And I could not move for twenty minutes. It often seemed like forever.

I got up onto the table in the usual manner and laid back. The assistant placed the mask very carefully over my face so as not to cause me pain. But they all knew what I knew. No matter how carefully they tried, it was going to hurt. They would always apologize when I winced

The Supernatural Power of His Presence

from the contact with the mask. I was all fastened in and ready to begin, hopefully, another uneventful treatment. The radiation itself never caused pain while being administered. It just silently and painlessly burnt my skin like an unseen tormentor.

Jesus Enters the Room

The machine engaged and I was centered inside the circular aperture. The machine wound up and began delivering the radiation. I was very familiar with the sounds the machine made throughout the process and could gauge fairly accurately how far along I was in the session by those sounds. On this particular day I remember feeling emotionally dejected and just plain fed up with it all. At this point I would have been fine with going home to heaven just so it all would end. Out of nowhere my spirit welled up inside me and I began to sing a song in my mind. I had not sung that song in years and yet the words came streaming back to me.

All of a sudden He entered the room. I didn't see Him, but I knew He was there. His manifest presence was overwhelming. I had experienced the presence of the Lord before but never to this magnitude. But what happened next was off the charts. It felt like He came over to the table and sat down on top of me in the very same way I did to get up on the table, only it seemed like He was on the opposite side from which I would mount the table. It was like He swung His left leg on top of my left leg followed by His right in the very same order that I mounted the table. Then it felt like He laid back and superimposed Himself into me and lay there within me. There are no words to sufficiently describe that moment.

> All of a sudden He entered the room. I didn't see Him, but I knew He was there. His manifest presence was overwhelming.

I could not feel Him physically but I could feel Him spiritually. He was in me, He was with me, and I was in Him. His presence was indescribably wonderful! It was all encompassing and swallowed up all my pain, fatigue, and dejection. I had no consciousness of suffering. I tried to feel for any measure of the suffering I had lived with constantly

CAPTURING THE SUPERNATURAL: HEALED!

over the past four months and I could not find it. It had been totally vanquished by the overwhelming glorious victory of His magnificent presence. I felt strong and whole as His life surged through my spirit, soul, and body. It was like nothing I had ever experienced before and may never experience again until I am in His presence forever. How long He stayed with me I do not know, but it was not long enough. His presence seemed to fill every cell of my being, but yet every cell cried for more. His presence was completely satisfying, yet I wanted more of Him. Nothing mattered at that point—He was enough! I could not feel any measure of guilt, shame, or sadness over my sin or any disappointment over the things I had done that could ever have caused Him pain. It was only sheer bliss and blessedness as I was filled with the fullness of joy of being in His manifest presence.

Then He sat up and dismounted the table in reverse order that He came and left the room. Surprisingly I did not feel sad. I was basking in the residual impartation of His visitation. I was rejoicing! In my spirit I had substantive faith, knowing I would come through my battle with cancer. The Lord did not physically heal me that day. However, He infused me with His manifest presence. He radiated my entire being with His glorious presence. He filled me with the Spirit and power of His might, strengthening me to fight on. As I reflected upon the whole encounter I realized how significant it was that He mounted the table the same way I did. He was letting me know that he had been there all along. He had been observing everything I had been experiencing, down to the smallest detail, even how I had to mount the table. Dear reader, He is always present with us. But He is not always visibly present with us. There is a day coming when He will be visibly present with us. We will live in His manifest presence for all eternity. I am convinced heaven will be heaven because of His manifest presence. Every tear will be wiped away, every fear vanquished, every sin, transgression, and iniquity ever committed will be completely removed from memory because of the overwhelming power of His manifest presence. This is the eternal destiny of all who put their faith in the Person and work of Jesus of Nazareth, the Son of God upon the cross, and His resurrection from the dead. All believers will live in the unity of faith and dwell forever in His supernatural manifest presence.

The Supernatural Power of His Presence

Strength for the Rest of the Battle

My encounter with His manifest presence gave me the strength to persevere to the end of my battle with cancer. I finished the chemo and radiation treatments on time. One additional treatment was also performed—brachytherapy, in which a very high concentration of radiated beads are delivered through tubes inserted into the tongue directly to the tumor area. This was done to ensure that no cancerous cell, missed by the radiation, survived. A PET scan was then scheduled to be conducted after a six-week period of rest and recovery to determine if all the treatments had been successful in destroying the tumor. It was such a relief not to be pierced, poked, or prodded by well-meaning doctors and assistants; not to have to spend countless hours traveling feeling like death warmed over; and to actually feel my body, mind, and spirit beginning to recover from the battle that had been waged in every part of my being. The PET scan revealed that the treatments had been successful, and the tumor was gone!

As I write, the fifth anniversary of my completion date approaches, which is an important milestone. After five years of continuous remission the patient is considered to be officially cured. I returned to my duties as a local pastor shortly after the treatments ended, which I continue to this day. The damage caused by the tumor and radiation treatments to my tongue remains. I cannot swallow solid food, so the feeding tube is still in place. And because I am unable to swallow, I must spit in a paper cup to remove saliva from my mouth. The mucus buildup is still there but is tolerable. My speech impediment remains although there has been significant improvement. These impediments will stay with me until the Lord heals them or I receive my new body. But Dr. K.'s prophetic declaration is now a reality! I preach the glorious gospel of Jesus Christ to this day. I teach His people His Word. I am alive and serving Him together with my courageous wife as we follow Him into our ultimate destiny—living with Him in His manifest presence for all eternity. And for that I will be eternally grateful for His goodness to me.

My encounter with the manifest presence of Jesus Christ has caused me to believe there is not a sadder or more dreaded Scripture verse than

Capturing the Supernatural: Healed!

2 Thessalonians 1:9. The apostle Paul is speaking about all who do not obey the gospel of Jesus Christ and declares they will be "punished with everlasting destruction *from the presence of the Lord and from the glory of His power"* (NKJV).

Scripture is clear that everyone will stand before Christ to receive final judgment. Can you imagine coming into the manifest presence of the Lord Jesus Christ, experiencing the overwhelming magnificence of His presence, and then being banished from the glory and the power of His presence for all eternity?

Dear readers, if you have not yet received Jesus Christ as your personal Savior, do so now. Do not wait another moment. Receive Him by faith today! He died as the atonement of your personal sin. Your debt to God has been paid by Jesus Christ. If you come to Him in sincere repentance and faith, He will not reject you. The blood of Jesus is so powerful it cleanses the worst of sin. He will accept you and give you His manifest presence as your eternal inheritance. For all those who have received Christ, continue in doing well; do not faint regardless of your circumstances. I assure you that dwelling in the weighty glory of His manifest presence outweighs the light afflictions that we suffer in this present world.

> **Gregory Bogart** has been in ministry for over twenty years. He has served as pastor of two churches. Gregory has ministered internationally in Canada, Ukraine, Czech Republic, and Haiti and is currently ministering in the US territory of Puerto Rico. Gregory and his wife Debra minister together preaching the good news of the gospel of Jesus Christ and the kingdom of God. Their passion is to equip and prepare the body of Christ for the great end-time harvest of souls. They have six children and seven grandchildren. Gregory can be contacted at watcherg12@gmail.com.

Right Where You Are

Kathy Dolman

Right Where You Are

Kathy Dolman

A large crowd followed and pressed around him. And a woman was there who had been subject to bleeding for twelve years. She had suffered a great deal under the care of many doctors and had spent all she had, yet instead of getting better she grew worse. When she heard about Jesus, she came up behind him in the crowd and touched his cloak, because she thought, "If I just touch his clothes, I will be healed." Immediately her bleeding stopped and she felt in her body that she was freed from her suffering (Mark 5:24-29).

"Oh please, not again…"

These were the words I said often. Too often. I was beginning to feel just like the woman with the issue of blood in Mark 5. I tried to deal the best I could with my female problem with as much discretion and decorum as I could muster. Having to deal with the sudden onset of the episodes and voraciousness of the problem was wearing on me. And it seemed it was getting worse with each passing month. There were times when I had to leave work or miss it altogether because of the severity of the problem. Much of my time was spent on trying to ensure I didn't have any embarrassing accidental moments. Then there was the financial cost from ruined clothing along with the need for a large supply of female products to cope with. I had a stash of "supplies" everywhere, just in case—tucked away at work, in my purse, I even had a spot in the trunk of my car where I buried supplies and a bag with extra clothes just in case.

Capturing the Supernatural: Healed!

My doctor assured me that there were many women who suffered with the same issue, especially as they got older. And the good news—he had just the procedure to end my suffering that was not invasive surgery! I remember saying with a big fat grin, "Sign me up!"

And so, a few weeks later, I entered the same-day surgery center at my local hospital and underwent the procedure under anesthesia. I woke up feeling fairly well and went home to rest. I was told in a day or two all the discomfort from the procedure would disappear and the bleeding problem would be greatly improved and possibly completely obliterated.

Strange Pain

On day three I called the doctor complaining of pain. It wasn't discomfort—it was pain. I was assured that it was normal and would improve. A few days later, to an extent, it did improve. The original problem was gone. The bleeding had completely stopped and I was able to go back to work. A new problem, however, had surfaced. I began to notice that when I stood for longer than just a few minutes, I got a pain that felt sort of like a muscle cramp but with a sharp edge to it. It was the same pain that I had experienced the first few days after the procedure, but now it felt like someone was tearing at the muscles in my lower abdomen. When I called the doctor again, I was told because the original issue was resolved that what I had was normal recovery, and with time it would resolve itself.

> It was the same pain that I had experienced the first few days after the procedure, but now it felt like someone was tearing at the muscles in my lower abdomen.

So, I waited. And waited. And waited. About a month or so later, I was still dealing with this strange pain. I couldn't sleep on the one side because any pressure to the lower abdominal area caused extreme discomfort. If I walked for long distances or stood for a period of time, I had to sit down to ease the pain.

Right Where You Are

A visiting minister was scheduled to hold a Sunday evening service at my church. I had never been in any of his meetings and I wasn't sure what to expect. He was a long-time evangelist that some of the older members of my church remembered from years past, and that he had a strong anointing for physical healing.

A Special Request

The meeting was fairly well attended. People with various physical ailments had come, and one by one the evangelist took their hands and walked them to the front of the church. There he would pray for them and the Lord's healing hand was evident.

It was now starting to get late as he continued to pray for folks. Each time he finished praying for one person, he would scan the pews and call out another. By this time, I had my head down and began to pray. I remember praying, "Lord, please. I know You are healing people through this man's gifting. You know I need to be healed. I don't want to live with this pain one more day. I know You can heal me right where I am. To be honest, Lord, I really wouldn't like to be brought up to the front like the others he is praying for. My issue is a bit embarrassing, especially since there are so many visitors here tonight. Yet I know Your healing power is here. So even though I'm not going to be pointed out by this man, I know You can heal me anyway."

As I finished my prayer, the minister stood in the middle aisle and said, "Well, folks, it's getting quite late. I know some of you may need to leave, being that it is a weeknight, and if you have to that's just fine. I need to take a quick break and get a drink, and if anyone can stay for prayer I will still be here."

Do You Believe?

I reached over to grab my keys and my Bible. And then I heard him say, "But! Before we take a break…you there! The woman in the back with the white shirt in the corner, would you stand please?"

Capturing the Supernatural: Healed!

He was looking right at me. I remember sighing, thinking to myself, "Oh Lord. Please don't let him ask me to come up front."

He stopped halfway up the middle aisle and said, "You have an issue with pain in your lower abdomen, don't you?"

I think I stopped breathing at this point. "Yes," I answered weakly.

"Do you believe that the Lord can heal you right where you are standing, without me laying a hand on you or calling you up front? Do you believe He can heal you right where you are?"

I remember choking back tears now. "Yes!" I said.

He asked me to raise my hands toward heaven and then said, "Right now the Lord is healing you from the problem you've had since you had that procedure done."

I was astonished. I hadn't said a word to him about having had a surgical procedure! I had never met this man before in my life!

He continued. "The doctor doesn't understand what's happening with you because what they don't know is that there is a tear inside that they have not discovered. If the Lord had not healed you tonight, you would be headed for another surgery. Come out in that rear aisle and walk around a bit. And I want you to do something else. I want you to take both hands and press really hard on the sides of your lower abdomen. Do you feel the pain?"

"No! The pain is gone!" I shouted. "The pain is gone!"

He Knows!

Even years later, every time I think about that night, I ponder not only the wonderful healing power of the Lord, but I also think about *the way* He healed me. He knew in my heart that I didn't want to be put in a spotlight at the front of the church. In His grace and His compassion and understanding of my personality, and in answer to my prayer, He performed a personalized miracle for me.

Right Where You Are

He healed me without moving out into the aisle. He healed me without walking to the front of the church where I would have been a bit embarrassed about my condition. He healed me without having so much as a finger being placed on me. He knew! He knew I didn't want to be paraded around, as it were. He knew, and He heard, and He did it! He did it right where I was!

I think that, beyond the fact that I was physically healed that night, having that sense of His personal, intimate knowledge and love for me has left me in awe. I'm not quite sure how to describe how I felt that night. What I mean to say is, I know that the Lord loves me. I've been taught it all my life, even before I turned my life over to Him. Yet this was tangible proof that He did love me. He did know me and saw all my needs. He did hear my prayer! The God who created the universe, countless galaxies, and countless stars cared enough about little ol' me to heal me in the way that most suited my comfort level, without fanfare and drama and display.

> He healed me without moving out into the aisle. He did it right where I was!

It's been years since that night. I'm still free from the original bleeding issue and from the pain. Whenever I get to a new trial in my life, I think back to that night and I'm reminded of His passionate love for me. I'm in awe of His power and His individual care of each of His children.

Kathy Dolman grew up in the Wyoming Valley of northeastern Pennsylvania as the youngest of seven children. From her earliest years, she has always enjoyed writing. Kathy holds a degree in journalism and has had articles published in local newspapers and *Pray!* magazine. Kathy is the author of *The Light at Hope's End* and *The Miracle at Hope's End*. A native of Swoyersville in northeastern Pennsylvania, Kathy currently resides in Dupont, Pennsylvania with her husband, Jerry, and two sons, Jerry Jr. and Kevin. She is an active member of the Full Gospel Chapel of Avoca. Kathy can be contacted at mom2times@hotmail.com.

For Freedom's Sake

Kathy Hill

For Freedom's Sake
Kathy Hill

At five years old, I found the beginning of new life. I was invited to attend vacation Bible school at a small church a couple of miles away from my house, and while I don't remember those very early days, my mom said it changed everything. She said she would hear the church bells ring down the street and feel as though her children needed to be in church. When a neighbor invited us that summer to VBS, it made the journey toward church easy for our family. By the age of eight, I had accepted Jesus as my personal Lord and Savior and been water baptized. Even as a child I loved working in the church and found that I never wanted to miss a service. As we drove onto the parking lot each Sunday, I can remember smiling as I felt "this was home."

I was raised to "know" Jesus and to love serving the family of God, but it would not be until many years later that I would come to a place of understanding about the true freedom only *knowing* Jesus would provide.

My remembrance of early church life, with all of its flamboyant and joy-filled family activities, would soon be overshadowed by the realistic sting that being overweight was a prison cell, especially for a child. Growing up as a "chubby," "big-boned," "healthy," "strapping" girl (as the old-timers would say) was a horrible sentence for any child and I could not imagine what I had done to make God or *life* entrap me with such bondage. I was the only child I knew eating homemade, sugar-free ketchup on toasted bread covered with garlic, mushrooms, and a slice of cheese to substitute for real pizza. Really? Quite honestly stomaching faux pizza was easier than trying to fit into a group of skinny people

Capturing the Supernatural: Healed!

when you absolutely were not one. Even as I reflect now, the sting of that feeling immediately stabs my heart. The only good thing about this was I could retreat to church where there was a safe place and the few other children in my Sunday school class were kind. Nobody had taught me how to handle my feelings of rejection, ridicule, and depression. So I ate.

The Prison of Obesity

Eating is a big deal to my family. I come from a long line of amazing cooks and hefty people who love family gatherings and are not ashamed to laugh out loud and celebrate the art of overeating. I not only love to eat, I love to eat a lot; and if you combine those traits with a mother who is an "off the chain" cook preparing to feed an army at each meal, being healthy became an unbeatable challenge. Of course, when I was young no one really spoke of high cholesterol or air-brushed models and eating was associated with pleasure.

The lunchroom ladies at my elementary school delighted in preparing the yummiest and most decadent lunches. It was almost a competition between the lunchrooms to see whose yeast rolls received the highest accolades. And can yeast rolls be eaten without butter running down the sides? No! In addition to stupendous home cooking and calorie-rich school lunches, there were the weekly church dinners. All the mothers of the church joined the weekly competition to see who could out-cook the rest. I, of course, joined the competition to see who could out-eat the rest. In those years, the president's wives didn't care if elementary children were chubby or not. Actually no one cared. That's not true—I cared.

> My prison of obesity was padded with a horrible self-image and a rotten jealousy that would lead me toward a path of destruction.

I was not stupid, and I was very aware that I wasn't shaped like the other girls. It seemed the more aware I became of this plight, the more trapped I felt. Not only was I different, but the others treated me differently. That was the real prison. My prison of obesity was padded with a horrible self-image and a rotten jealousy that would lead me toward a path of destruction. Wanting to be somebody you're not and loathing anyone who is that person is torment. I was trapped and tormented all the time, and I was just turning thirteen. Life was not supposed to be like this, but this was my reality. Then the hiding started.

The deeper my unhappiness reached, the faster I grabbed and hid food in places where no one would realize the truth. Given the choice of faux pizza or a box of cookies, which would you choose? The only issue with hiding food is that one's body doesn't hide extravagant consumption well. The more I consumed, the more my body displayed, the angrier and more frustrated I became that *I would never be free.* Never.

When I entered high school, my desire to be popular was consuming. It appeared that all my friends were the popular ones and I was the heavy one. I had tried multiple times and in multiple ways to manage this horror house. Failure was my constant companion. However, I did have a friend who was a majorette and really encouraged me to try out. At first the thought of failing again—especially in light of not making the cheerleading squad, as I was too chunky to do splits or turn cartwheels—was daunting. However, being a majorette was more like dancing and my friend assured me the coach was easy. That's when my journey changed drastically.

In the "Skinny Girl" Group

I began to practice the routine to be used for tryouts day and night. I was determined to make this squad. I never put the baton down and I played the song for hours practicing and perfecting. What happened was amazing to me. The more I practiced, the smaller I got. The smaller I got, the more I practiced. Then it happened—the knock on the door—the senior girls shouting, "You made it. We've come to kidnap you for initiation." Could this really be happening?

Making the squad meant lots of practice and tiny costumes, which equaled *no eating* for me. For the first time, I was in the "skinny girl" group. Some girls could eat all they wanted and remain in that group. But for me, I stopped hiding food to eat at a later time and began hiding

Capturing the Supernatural: Healed!

food so others would think I had eaten when I had not. I developed an eating disorder and was still in prison. I had transferred cells, but found myself with a different set of chains. Medically this lifestyle took its toll, and I eventually began eating again as opposed to being hospitalized. It was horrible! I never came to the realization that food was designed to give life; I simply stopped expecting life at all.

I started gaining weight, again, and decided to leave high school at the end of my junior year for college as I felt I was no longer in the "skinny girl" group and no longer belonged. Once away at school where no one cared if I ate or didn't, I chose eating. It was my happy place… for a moment.

At this age I was more aware of prayer and expecting God to answer prayer and yet, in my opinion, He never answered *mine*. I prayed diligently for God to make me skinny, popular, take away my love for food, and bring happiness even for a moment. What I really wanted was for God to allow me to eat everything I desired while wearing a size two. I tried every spiritual tactic I knew. I pleaded, begged, cried, shouted the Scriptures, and was still hopelessly trapped. The longer God delayed responding to my plea, the more anger my heart gathered. The bad part about anger is that it can fester for long periods of time. However, if not properly dealt with, anger eventually emerges as an ugly monster from a deep shadow. College and late night pizza added pounds upon pounds and once again I had resolved within myself that prison was my portion. Although I had memorized Scriptures about freedom, I internalized that I could never walk in it myself.

The Crash

Following college, I returned home and immediately secured a teaching job that I loved! Teaching was exciting except for the fact that I was forty pounds heavier than when I left for college. I started back through a journey of starvation accompanied with a huge sense of failure—again. Once again my body responded with shedding the extra pounds, and within a short period of time I was dating and introduced to the idea of taking speed to deal with the frustration of being overweight.

For Freedom's Sake

Drugs seemed to be the immediate answer, and I found myself trapped, again, but in a different padded cell. The only issue with taking drugs to lose weight was that I never learned the value of life and believing God to fill my body with the foods He created to sustain life, nor the plan He had established for me. This "drug" journey worked in my mind, as I didn't have to pray, trust God, or starve. I was in constant motion and never hungry—until the crash.

I would love to say that this was a singular, life-defining crash that would change the course of my young adult life. But it was not! Marriage, childbirth, miscarriages, and the pressures of living in a difficult marriage with a child who was born with a chronically deformed heart finally pushed me to the brink of desperation. *Desperation without God is hopelessness beyond explanation.* I no longer had God as my retreating place because I had wandered away from my faith in Him the last couple of years of college and for ten long years had lived my life as the prodigal daughter.

> Desperation without God is hopelessness beyond explanation.

Without any inner hope of returning to God, I reached to every imaginable alternative to help with the pain of feeling trapped. I went back to taking speed, was hypnotized, took shots, was sprayed with solutions and wrapped for hours, slept in belts, took a second kind of speed, used positive confession and yoga techniques to gain my freedom; this was a never-ending horror story. However, God never gave up on me and continued to reach out to me through various distinct and strategic encounters. One amazing night, I surrendered my heart to the Lordship of Jesus Christ anew and began a marvelous journey toward the freedom I now embrace.

Overcoming the Giants

Those who have suffered through emotional prison cells of obesity and obesity-related diseases know the next segment of my journey. Although I had returned home to my faith, I still had the unfortunate reality that "giants" remained in *my land*. How could this be? I had

Capturing the Supernatural: Healed!

suffered enough and now my body was responding to my past with illnesses that required legal medications. Each year brought an additional ailment as well as new medications. While I had recommitted my life to Jesus, I was still a voracious eater and not a healthy one—at all. It seemed I was disciplined in almost every area of my life except in the area of health. My constant prayer and plea was for deliverance in my body and mind. I knew that God's best for my body was to walk in health and be free of these chronic ailments that had begun to rob me of life, but the struggle for freedom was relentless. Prayer and studying the Word of God became my passion, as it seemed to be my only hope.

I stumbled across Galatians 5:1, which would become the truth upon which my freedom from the obesity prison would be established. "It is for freedom that Christ came to set me free; I will stand firm then *and no longer let myself be burdened again with a yoke of slavery."* As I researched and studied this passage, I understood the context and the biblical meaning conveyed. The converted Jews were being challenged to commit themselves to the regulations of the Law. However, the apostle Paul was teaching them that their relationship with Jesus was not determined by the physical act of being circumcised but through the circumcision of their hearts. This had caused an uproar with the Jewish leaders, and some of the new converts were retreating. They had not learned to stand in their newly gained freedom, which Christ had purchased and presented to them. They had not fully connected with the truth that each of them had a part to play on their *freedom* journey, which was to stand in *the* truth. I finally understood.

According to Galatians 5:1 Jesus purchased my freedom from eternal death, but I had a responsibility to *stand and maintain* that freedom. This truth finally clicked. Additionally, I came to embrace that Jesus died to give me freedom in every area of my life. Jesus completed His portion of the equation, and the greater challenge, in my heart, was to complete mine. I understood and yet I felt as though I had no strength to stand against an enemy that had controlled my life for fifty-four years. I had no pattern to assist me with standing. This prompted an intense study in the only manual I knew that offered truth that would overcome all obstacles—the Bible.

For Freedom's Sake

The best biblical example I could find to study and dissect, as a means of fashioning my weapon, was found in the book of Exodus. The children of Israel suffered and endured chronic hardships for four hundred years and cried with a loud voice for God to deliver them. Not only did He send a deliverer, He created a path and a plan by which His promise to Abraham would be fulfilled. God never reneges on His promises. He said that Abraham's descendants would be as numerous as the stars and cover the earth. God's Word is steadfast. However, as the children of Israel left Egypt and headed toward their Promised Land, the enemy came to ensure their destruction. God, once again, brought the steadying of His Word through His servant Moses to give the people courage to continue. Exodus 14:13-14 declares, *"Moses answered the people, 'Do not be afraid. Stand firm and you will see the deliverance the Lord will bring you today. The Egyptians you see today you will never see again. The Lord will fight for you; you need only to be still.'"*

The acceptance and firm commitment of this verse in my life rocked my world. How amazing are those two verses? Standing firm in the freedom that was purchased and provided for me became my immediate determination. I knew I would stand; I could see it now. However, I had yet to be delivered. I knew without the Spirit of the Lord coming and breaking this lifelong addiction to an unhealthy lifestyle, my declaration to stand would be in vain.

Sweet Deliverance

On January 24th, 2011, filled with truth and hope, I prayed what I felt would be my final plea for deliverance. I really felt as if this was the end of me and the beginning of true freedom. On that day, God supernaturally and sovereignly delivered me from an addiction that had kept me in prison my entire life. Truth and revelation flooded my soul with a joy that is almost indescribable. Over the next nine months I learned to enjoy real foods for the first time and the taste of water. Additionally I lost sixty-five pounds, which have never returned. That may seem trite, but to someone who was unhealthy, obese, and taking a handful of medications every morning for obesity-related illnesses, the simplicity of eating as God planned has been liberating. Not only did my weight find its healthy place, my blood and internal organs began to heal themselves. Within weeks I was no longer taking medications for reflux, arthritis, diabetes, and cholesterol. The blood pressure medicine I had taken for thirty years had been cut in half. I could not believe the miraculous hand of God!

I made a commitment to God on that January morning, based off weeks of research, to never eat starch or sugar again and God absolutely delivered me. Sugar and starch find their way into almost every processed food in American culture and often under hidden names. A quick study of labels on most readily available, processed foods will support this. And while these two outlaws seem to offer the taste that we so desperately *feel* we need and want, they are silently undermining God's best plan for our bodies. Sugar and starch were my giants and had to be eliminated; as they stood tall in my promised land, God delivered me and I was determined to stand. Standing, for me, meant I would never use or eat them again. In my deliverance, God not only broke their hold in my body as He gave me the courage to say "never" and mean it, but He also gave me an excellent sense of taste for even the tiniest amount of sugar. People are amazed at how discerning my sense of taste is. It's totally God!

Years of being healthy, for the first time in my life, have given me the hope and assurance that this physical body will not keep me from fulfilling the call of God on my life. God delivered me and I embarked on the freedom journey, which meant my way of doing life had to change. With God's supernatural help I closed a door that cold, January day that I never intend to open again. I don't even walk close to that door or embrace the lie of "all things in moderation." I never leave anything to chance. I call ahead when eating at a party to see if my hostess has prepared anything that I can eat. I only eat at restaurants that support my healthy lifestyle. I have changed holiday meals for my family, and everyone who knows me *knows* that starch and sugar are never allowed to be giants in my life again. God said *to stand* and I *am standing* in the miraculous deliverance He has provided. As God established my path to freedom, He commissioned me to turn and help others embrace a healthy lifestyle as well. This was the motivation to write a devotional cookbook called *Apples, Brownies, or Both?*

God has a plan for the gospel to be spread throughout the earth. His plan clearly states that Jesus is the only method for salvation and this is a free gift. And yes, Jesus did purchase our freedom and provide the gift, but our adversary and the circumstances of life are forever in pursuit of and robbing and stealing the hope and promises of God for His followers. I am committed to stand guard and *never allow myself to be burdened again with a yoke of slavery* (see Galatians 5:1b). For me, that's a miracle!

Kathy Hill is an example of what happens when southern hospitality combines with the supernatural personality of the Holy Spirit. She's an inspirational communicator who regularly instructs through her personal and poignant blog posts. Equal parts inquisitive student, inspirational teacher, and persistent coach, Kathy eagerly shares personal experiences, practical examples, and biblical truths to encourage us to live a victorious Christian life. Currently, Kathy serves as Executive Pastor at New City Church in the Atlanta, Georgia area and oversees staff, ministry teams, weekend services, and events. She is also a prolific blogger, personal coach, wife, mother, grandmother, and speaker. Kathy is the author of the devotional cookbook *Apples, Brownies, or Both?*. Find out more about Kathy at www.freedomconnection.org.

HEALED!

Chronic No More

Cathy Sanders

CHRONIC NO MORE

Cathy Sanders

Faith is the confidence that what we hope for will actually happen; it gives us assurance about things we cannot see (Hebrews 11:1 NLT).

What's wrong with me? I thought as I shoved another cough drop in my mouth in a vain attempt to try and ward off another coughing fit. Knowing I was supposed to sing in just a few minutes didn't help the matter. In fact, concentrating on *not* coughing made me feel like I had to cough all the more. It seemed like this cold, if that's what it was, had been dragging on forever and was prohibiting my main purpose in life—to glorify God through singing and leading worship. What I didn't realize was that it wasn't a cold I was dealing with. The next trip to the doctor would confirm that I was dealing with severe allergies for which I would have to take medicine every day of my life if I wanted to pursue a career in music.

Here, Kitty, Kitty

For as long as I can remember I have had some sort of problem with allergies. When I was young it would rear its ugly head whenever I was around cats. I remember having itchy, puffy eyes whenever I was at a friend's house who owned a feline companion, and it didn't take long from the moment I stepped into her house until I started feeling the effects. As an animal lover it was irresistible for me to not pet the fuzzy creature rubbing its body against my leg. As much as I would try to keep my hands out of my eyes, they would still get red, watery, and

Capturing the Supernatural: Healed!

itchy, soon to be followed by sneezing along with constricted breathing until I was completely miserable.

I can recall one Christmas that we went to my aunt and uncle's house instead of having the whole family squeeze into our home again as usual. I had not been to my aunt and uncle's place in a long time so I didn't know they had a cat. This time I didn't even pet the kitty and within a few hours of arriving, the itching started. Talk about a miserable Christmas Day! I could not wait to go home and wash all the bothersome dander off my face and body.

To top it off, one of the few presents that I got to open that day were three pairs of bright neon knee-high socks. This came at a time when neon was *not* popular. I said thank you but internally scratched my head, wondering why. Being a resourceful person, I found a great use for the socks in the wintertime. I wore them under normal colored socks for an extra layer of warmth. What's even better is that the socks didn't make my eyes itch.

I had thought that my allergic problem was just limited to cats until one summer in my high school years when I decided to get a job working at the local thrift store sorting the donated clothes. My job was to separate the good clothes that could be sold from the garments that were too far gone to be worth anything. Unfortunately the room—and all the clothes—was very dusty; dust particles were everywhere. We had to wear gloves and masks to prevent breathing in the mold and mildew all day. But even these small precautions didn't stop the dust from affecting me. What a job I picked as my first introduction to the work force, right? By the time I went home I could barely breathe and my eyes were painfully red and swollen. It didn't take very long (I'm pretty sure it was less than a week or two) to figure out that this was not the job for me. As much as I hated not finishing something I had started, I had to quit and find a summer job that wouldn't fill my lungs with dust and send my eyes into red itching madness.

Time went by and I managed to stay away from cats of any kind and also from any place that might send my allergies into a frenzy. I was able to avoid any really horrible reactions through college and into the first years of my married life with my wonderful husband, Andy.

CHRONIC NO MORE

Chronic Cough

When our second child, Joselyn, was about a year old we became pastors of a church not too far away from Chicago, Illinois. I could use my talents in music more in this position than anywhere in the past as I was leading worship, conducting the church choir for special holiday services, and writing and composing my own songs and worship music on the side. I was living a dream—to be able to devote so much time to my family, the church, and music.

After we had lived there for a while, I developed a respiratory sickness that I just couldn't seem to shake. It seemed like a cold from which I just could not recover. I took cough medicine, sucked on cough drops, and tried any over-the-counter solutions I could find to no avail. I went to the doctor and instead of a sickness, he said that it was an allergy, stating that a lot of people in the area got it because of all the factories and poor air quality. He said there was a chance it could be seasonal and that maybe in the winter when all the pollen was removed out of the air, it would get better. For now he suggested that I start taking an allergy medicine once a day and prepare to deal with it for the long haul.

The medicine took a few weeks to fully take effect and then I was able to function close to normal, except in times where I needed to sing for extended periods of time. Then my throat got very irritated and normally I ended up in a coughing fit. It was hard to deal with as a singer (beside the fact that it was not very professional and downright embarrassing to hack up your lungs right on stage in front of the whole congregation). I started praying for God to heal me, at the same time wondering if this was my "thorn in the flesh" like Paul had to endure.

And lest I should be exalted above measure by the abundance of the revelations, a thorn in the flesh was given to me, a messenger of Satan to buffet me, lest I be exalted above measure (2 Corinthians 12:7 NKJV).

Winter came and I decided to go off the medicine to see if it was a seasonal allergy, but it came right back in force within a few days. It seemed there would be no end to this condition! It was not only

CAPTURING THE SUPERNATURAL: HEALED!

bothersome to me, but also to my family. I was constantly coughing. My husband is a light sleeper, so many times I would have to leave the comfort of our bedroom and sleep somewhere else in the house at night so he could get some rest. I didn't like it, but it seemed like I would have to take medicine every day of my life unless God healed my condition. I reluctantly started the medicines again.

> It was so difficult to have the thing that I knew was my life's calling cut short because of a physical issue that was out of my control.

Being healed from these chronic allergies became a key petition—one I took to the Lord again and again from that time on. I prayed, asked, begged, pleaded, and whined to the Lord to take the allergies away. I stood in prayer lines and asked close friends to pray with me for my healing. I figured the more people I asked, the greater the chance that I would get healed, right? Wrong. I started feeling that it would never end. It was so difficult to have the thing that I knew was my life's calling cut short because of a physical issue that was out of my control.

On the Road

In June 2006, our family prepared to go out on the road, traveling and ministering wherever God would lead us. It was a faith-filled adventure. We spent the next four years ministering full time with our kids. We had a large RV we pulled behind our truck for us to live in because we would be out on the road for up to eight months at a time before coming home to rest and recharge for the next trip.

Living by faith is both scary and wonderful at the same time. There were weeks when we wondered where provision would be coming from next, and although we tried as hard as we could to schedule weeks and months in advance, there were times we did not know from one week to the next where we would end up.

All through our travels, dotting across the country and even into other countries, we saw God perform miracle after miracle for many, many people who were hungry for the presence of God. Our services often lasted for hours beyond the normal ending time because God was not done yet. People did not want to leave; they were sometimes simply engulfed in the presence of God that poured out at our services. I usually played and sang, worshipping until there were just a few people left so as not to interrupt what God was doing in people's hearts. Countless people were touched and changed by God's Spirit as my husband ministered and as I played and sang.

Still through all of the amazing things I saw God doing for other people, I still had to deal daily with severe chronic allergies. I was hoping that once I got away from the area that we used to live in that the allergy problem would clear up and I would be fine, but every time I tried to go off the medicine it would come right back. There were times that I had to work around having a coughing fit in the middle of a song, which is not easy to deal with, especially when you are a professional ministry that a pastor is bringing in for the first time. The first impression I made on a few churches probably was not the best that it could have been because of the allergies I was dealing with.

Faith in Action

In April of 2008, I was invited to lead some worship for a conference near our hometown. We planned to be home around that time to celebrate Easter with my mom and dad anyway, so it fit perfectly into our traveling plans. Some of the people who were brought in to speak at this meeting were good friends of ours, so we looked forward to our time with them. After several powerful services I was talking with our friend who had come from another state to minister in the conference and happened to mention that I wished that I didn't have to deal with the allergies all the time. I wished that God would heal me. He immediately spoke up and said that his wife, who had traveled to the conference with him, had been healed of multiple allergy issues. He explained that because she had already experienced healing in that area, she had the faith to pray for others to be healed from allergy problems as well. He called her over along with several other women and girls who were present, and they gathered around me and began to pray for my healing.

I didn't feel anything spectacular when they prayed. There was no fire from heaven, no lights, no burning sensation, nothing to indicate

Capturing the Supernatural: Healed!

> I made a decision that I was sick and tired of living on medicine to function in my calling and that I was going to believe that I was healed.

that I had been healed. In fact, I felt no different after they prayed than I did before, but something in my determination had changed. I made a decision that I was sick and tired of living on medicine to function in my calling and that I was going to believe that I was healed. Then I took it a step further. I also decided to act on my faith and stop taking the daily medication I was using to control the allergies.

Normally I would never condone anyone to go off of their medication, especially if it was a medication prescribed by a doctor for their health and wellbeing. If you feel that God has healed you, please talk with your doctor to find a safe way to test your healing and to prove that God has touched your body. In this situation, the doctor I originally went to with the diagnosis was several hundred miles away and we did not have health insurance, so I couldn't just go have a checkup anytime I wanted without paying out of pocket. I also knew that if I went off the medication and found that it was not the time for my healing, I would not be putting my life at risk; it would set me back a few weeks but I would eventually get back to my not-so-normal routine.

If there is one thing I have learned about faith, it is that faith requires action in order to work. It is like building a machine and hoping it will do what you created it to do without ever plugging it in or turning it on. Sometimes the problem is not that we don't have enough faith, it's that we don't act on it. We never step out of the boat to see if the water will hold us up; we don't reach out and touch the hem of Jesus' garment. James 2:17 says, "So also faith, if it does not have works (deeds and actions of obedience to back it up), by itself is destitute of power (inoperative, dead)" (AMP).

As I left the church that day, I decided that I would not take my allergy medication the next morning like normal. For the first several days after that, I held my breath while at the same time thanking God for healing me. After a few weeks of not experiencing any of the problems I used to encounter, I rejoiced that God had truly healed me. I was chronic no more!

Chronic No More

Tested

The ultimate test of my healing came less than a month later when we went to a ministry gathering in Florida. Sometimes when we travel we stay at a hotel, and other times we stay with a friend if they live close by. Doing this allows us to enjoy times of fellowship with people we don't get to see very often. We contacted our dear friends to let them know we would be in the area and asked if they might have a place for us to crash for a few nights. They were all too happy to welcome us into their home.

We arrived at the airport, secured our rental vehicle, and headed to our friend's home. What we didn't realize is that this family had several cats. And these weren't the nice little short-haired cats; they had long, soft fur that seemed to be shedding constantly. You could see the cat hair billowing in the corners of rooms, creating little tumbleweed-like fuzz balls rolling about on the ground. I knew I was healed, but had not expected to have my healing tested this quickly, or to this extreme! If we had known about the cats we may have leaned toward staying in a hotel. But being the good friends and guests that we were, we smiled and thanked our hosts for their hospitality and spent some time with them before heading off to the service that night. After an extended service with a lot of prayer and worship that went close to the midnight hour, we returned to our host's home.

That night I slept on a bed covered with cat hair; it was even on my pillow (I could have sworn the blanket on our bed was made from woven cat hair, I just can't prove that one). If the sun shone through the window just right you could see tufts of feather-light fur drifting happily along through the air. Before I had been healed there was no possible way I could have stayed in this home. We would have been forced to leave and find a hotel or some other accommodations so I could simply breathe, not to mention the disfigurement of my face from swelling and itching.

I remember one moment when my eyes tried to get itchy once, but I spoke to them and said, "Oh, no, you don't; I've been healed and you will no longer get affected by allergies anymore!"

Capturing the Supernatural: Healed!

My husband was truly convinced that I had been divinely healed when we woke up the next day with a cat in our room (he says it was even sleeping on the end of the bed) and I was fine. This was truly a test of my healing.

God not only healed me from chronic allergies. He also did it without me falling on the ground or feeling heat or some other physical sensation. Sometimes God wants to heal us, but we need to show how much we believe Him by acting on our faith. He is an awesome, good God who is waiting to heal His children. Step out of the boat, grab His hem, and give feet to your faith!

Cathy Sanders has been involved with music ministry since she was a teenager. She and her husband, Andy, met at college and married in 1994. A few years later she started writing and recording her own contemporary and worship songs and was later offered a fully-funded nationwide radio campaign from a music promotions company based in Nashville, Tennessee. Her music was played on the radio regularly for five years. After traveling for several years in ministry, the Sanders founded 5 Fold Media, a Christian-based publishing company, in 2009, where Cathy has worked full time as the project manager for over one hundred titles. Cathy has a BA from Central Bible College, and a Masters and Doctorate in Christian Education from Freedom Seminary, graduating with honors. Andy and Cathy travel and minister and reside in New York with their two children. Find out more about Cathy at www.andycathysanders.com.

OUT OF A COMA

Gary Auten

OUT OF A COMA

Gary Auten

Comatose

I woke up in the middle of the night bumping into walls, crashing into furniture, and eventually falling onto the bathroom floor. The noise startled my mom as she came to see what was happening. I was babbling and confused about where I was and what was happening to me. I was nine years old, and just the week before I had received a DPT immunization. Due to unforeseen circumstances the DPT would have a negative effect on my brain. My parents quickly rushed me to the hospital in Bradenton, Florida. Shortly after arriving, I began having severe seizures. The doctors had never seen anything like it. For two hours they gave me medicines, trying to calm my brain and keep me from having more seizures. After several hours of seizures, I was exhausted and my mom was exhausted. My body began to shut down, and I slipped into a coma.

I was in a coma for three days. My mother was in the hallway of the hospital lying across several chairs with a Bible open beside her. My mom is the youngest of fourteen kids and grew up in poverty. Her childhood was challenging, to say the least. Her earliest recollections of faith were in a small Pentecostal church that she went to and sat in the front row. The people were nice and she always enjoyed the music. Although she was not necessarily raised to know God, her faith was established in that little church in the front row. I remember a large family Bible always proudly displayed in our living room. We never really talked about God and rarely attended church, but I always had

CAPTURING THE SUPERNATURAL: HEALED!

an understanding that God was near. As she lay there in that hallway exhausted, she offered a prayer to God. "God, You can have my son, if You just wake him up."

The Mystery Nurse

I believe that God hears and answers the prayers of the desperate. Hannah was desperate, cried out for a son, and God heard her. Rachel was desperate, cried out for a son, and God heard her. That night I believe that God heard the plea of a desperate mother for her son. Just a few moments later, someone who was dressed like a nurse awakened her. My mom was tired and groggy, trying to listen to what she had to say. The nurse told my mom, "You need to take your son to Gainesville, Florida," and gave her a specific doctor's name. As they walked toward the nurse's station, my mom turned to thank the nurse and she was gone. When describing the woman to the nurse at the station, there was no one who fit that description who worked at that hospital. Although it has not been confirmed, both my mom and I believe that it was an angel. After consulting the doctors, they agreed that I should be moved. Two hours later they transferred me by ambulance to Gainesville Medical Center and to the exact doctor the "angel" had suggested.

I arrived in poor condition. I was in a coma and the doctors had no idea what was wrong with me. Two hours after arriving, the lead physician came to my parents and informed them that I had suffered major brain damage. He showed them the part of my brain that was dark and no longer functioning. He told them that if I woke up I would be paralyzed and would not be able to speak or take care of myself. They didn't expect me to wake up. My parents were devastated. The doctors gave them no hope of any real recovery. They diagnosed me with encephalitis, which is an acute

> He told them that if I woke up I would be paralyzed and would not be able to speak or take care of myself. They didn't expect me to wake up. My parents were devastated.

inflammation of the brain. I lay in a coma for two weeks in Gainesville, Florida. There was no good news, no hope of recovery; they were simply waiting to see what my body would do. They had taken an x-ray of my brain that clearly showed a large, dark, inactive area in my brain. Everything that had happened up to this point was very discouraging.

My parents were overwhelmed. Their son's life was hanging in the balance, and they had no way of affecting the outcome. When tragedy comes to a family's door it reveals the core of who they are and what they believe. My father was not a religious man. I can only remember attending church a handful of times. Any talk of God in our family reflected the belief that He was far away and not really involved in our lives. My dad's grandmother, who was a faithful Christian, always told him he was called to the ministry, an opinion with which my father didn't agree. My great-grandmother could apply pressure to my dad like no one I had ever seen. I know she prayed for him and his family. My sister sometimes went and spent summer vacations with her that were always filled with church events. I didn't quite understand everything, but I knew that when we sat down to eat at my great-grandmother's house, her simple prayer always moved me. *"The effective, fervent prayer of a righteous man avails much"* (James 5:16 NKJV).

Persistant Prayer

When my great-grandmother prayed for my dad and his family, I believe that God heard her prayers. Prayer isn't limited to time and space. A prayer that is offered today may not be answered for a generation or more. Prayer isn't a brief puff of smoke that quickly disappears. Prayer is eternal. A prayer is a request to God, heard by God, and never forgotten by God. When a prayer of sincerity reaches the ears of God, He honors that prayer with an answer. The answer may not arrive for minutes, hours, days, months, or years. But rest assured, the answer is coming. Proverbs 15:29 says, *"The Lord is far from the wicked, But He hears the prayer of the righteous"* (NKJV), and 1 Peter 3:12 says, *"For the eyes of the Lord are on the righteous, and His ears*

CAPTURING THE SUPERNATURAL: HEALED!

are open to their prayers" (NKJV). God hears and answers the prayers of those who call upon Him.

It took over 400 years of praying before the answer came in the form of Moses leading the children of Israel out of bondage. Daniel prayed and fasted twenty-one days before his answer arrived. By the time Jesus arrived, they had been praying for hundreds of years for His advent. It's fantastic when prayer is answered instantly. Everyone loves a quick answer for what they need. My sons, especially when they were young, were often impatient and wanted everything immediately. Prayer can be answered right away, but often prayer is a journey of patience and persistence. The mother who prays for a wayward child may not get to see that child return to the Lord in her lifetime. The one carrying disease may not get the healing they so desperately desire. Does that mean we stop praying? God forbid! Our prayer is the proof that we believe that God is greater than any test, trial, or trouble that we face. My prayer, in the face of my biggest challenge, speaks volumes toward what I really believe.

> Our prayer is the proof that we believe that God is greater than any test, trial, or trouble that we face.

In Luke 11:5-8 Jesus tells the story of the friend who comes at midnight asking for help. The man within refused because of the late hour and inconvenience. Yet, because of his persistence the friend receives what he was asking for. The midnight hour is synonymous with desperation and a plea for help. When the cancer won't go away, it's the midnight hour. When the addiction is consuming you, it's the midnight hour. When your marriage is near divorce, it's the midnight hour. This is the time to ask, seek, and knock (see Luke 11:9-10). Your prayer at the midnight hour proves that your faith isn't dormant but clinging to the hope of your heart, the Lord.

Answered Prayer

My parents were looking at their nine-year-old son in a coma with virtually no hope of any recovery. I believe that the prayer of my great-grandmother was hovering over my life, waiting for an opportunity. I believe that when my mother prayed that prayer of dedication, the answer was dispatched with great haste. Heaven had heard the prayer of a desperate great-grandmother and a broken mother. What power was released! For two weeks I was motionless, giving no signs of hope. Approximately fourteen days went by and not one time did the doctors say they saw any improvement. In the early morning hours while my mother was sleeping in the waiting room, a nurse came with great urgency, saying "Mrs. Auten, you need to come to your son's room immediately!" My mom's knees were literally buckling under the stress of what she thought was happening. The nurse, in her excitement, didn't inform my mom what had happened. She thought something terrible had taken place. When she walked into the room, I was sitting up in bed and telling everyone how hungry I was. My mom fell to the floor in disbelief that her son was awake and talking to her. I had some side effects of the coma, but they lasted only a few hours.

When your answered prayer is talking back to you face to face, it's overwhelming. I can imagine the turmoil that Thomas had when Jesus showed up and proved Himself to him. The other disciples had already informed him that Jesus had risen. Thomas wasn't convinced. He had to see it and feel it for himself. Jesus didn't rebuke Thomas for his "show me" attitude. He proved Himself to Thomas by saying "see and feel" what has happened. Although my mom had prayed, when the answer came, it was almost unbelievable.

The lead physician was called immediately. When the doctor arrived, he couldn't believe his eyes. For the next twenty-four hours, they did extensive testing on me in an effort to understand what had happened and why I was talking to them. The next day the doctor told my parents that he was a Christian man and had never seen anything like this. He sat down next to them, grabbed my mother's hand, while holding the brain x-ray with the dark spot and looked at my parents with tears in his eyes and said, "This is a miracle! There is no medical explanation for why your son is seemingly healed." His next words

CAPTURING THE SUPERNATURAL: HEALED!

stunned them. "You can take him home. We can't find anything wrong with him."

> We call it supernatural because God is super and we are natural. The miracle happens when God's "super" touches our "natural."

When God heals someone, we often call it a miracle or supernatural. You won't find the word "supernatural" in most Bible translations. We call it supernatural because God is super and we are natural. The miracle happens when God's "super" touches our "natural." The doctors and hospital staff were doing everything in their "natural" power to help me recover. They recognized that there was nothing in the natural world that could help me. Something "super" was going to have to intervene. Prayer is the invitation for the super to get involved in our natural. God receives the invitation and sends the answer. My great-grandmother, who prayed earnestly, never got to see the answer to her prayer. The super of God was eager to touch something natural. In the beginning of time the Spirit of God was hovering over the waters, waiting to affect something natural. I believe that the Holy Spirit is hovering over lives today—waiting for an invitation to get involved. Whatever you are facing in the natural, God has a "super" for it! The "super" of God healed my "natural" body. Truly, a supernatural miracle had taken place and no one could deny it.

Over the next few months the doctors, because of fear that seizures would return, prescribed medication for me. My body rejected the medicine, and I told my parents I didn't need it. They took me back to Gainesville Medical Center for more tests. The last words I ever heard the doctor say were, "Go play football!" and I did.

My testimony is that when people pray with sincerity, God hears and answers their prayer. The answer may not come in the package you expect or want. You might have to endure some pain and difficulty. I pray that your answer comes quickly. In case it doesn't, keep on asking, keep on seeking, and keep on knocking!

OUT OF A COMA

Gary Auten accepted Christ as his Savior when he was sixteen. He graduated from World Harvest Bible College in 1995 and has been a pastor for twenty years. Gary and his wife, Kimber, have been married for twenty-three years and reside in Evansville, Indiana where they pastor Cornerstone Church. Their three sons, Isaac, Seth, and Adam work side by side with them in the ministry. They have a passion for the manifest presence of God, and they want to impact others for Christ and be a testimony of the supernatural to all who will listen. Find out more about Gary at www.evansvillecornerstone.com.

The Best Mother on Earth

Bill Yount

The Best Mother on Earth
Bill Yount

Mom made us go to church. "You are going," she said. "As long as you are under our roof, you will be under the roof of God's house!"

Before I knew the Lord, I thanked Him that our church had a balcony. It didn't matter to Mom where we sat as long as we got under that roof. We perched on the highest and farthest seats from the pulpit. We talked and carried on with friends and got away with a lot of things, or so we thought.

Then one Sunday morning a lady from the pulpit started to sing, "He Touched Me." I suddenly discovered how long God's arm is. It's at least as long as the pulpit is from the balcony, for He touched me.

I rose from my friends and with weak knees started down the side steps of the balcony. I walked down the center aisle of the church, while she was still singing, making my way to the altar. I gave my life to the Lord that day, and I have never been the same since.

At eleven years old, Mom saw a huge goiter instantly disappear from my grandmother's neck in a Kathryn Kuhlman meeting. The next second a five-year-old boy beside her started jumping up and down, screaming, "Mommy, where are you? Where are you, Mommy?"

The mother standing right beside him said, "Honey, I am right here!"

Mom saw that little boy jump up into his mother's arms to see her for the first time as he shouted, "Oh, Mommy, I can see you! I can see you, Mommy!"

The mother began to cry out, "He was born blind!"

Capturing the Supernatural: Healed!

From that moment, my mother got this mindset: "This is the way my life is going to be," and it has been—for ninety years. Little did she know what she experienced in those miracle meetings would one day cause healing to run in her own life and family.

The Great Physician

Mom had cancer thirty-five years ago. It was spreading through her body with the death sentence of five years. She felt led to visit a different church in town. She went with Aunt Sophie who had been healed so many times that people thought she was crazy. If you are believing for a miracle or healing, be careful who you spend your time with. You better find two or three crazy people who believe "all things are possible"!

My mom and Aunt Sophie arrived early and sat near the front of the church before others got there. As soon as Mom sat down, she felt a hand touch her shoulder, shooting a bolt of electricity down through her body and burning the hairs off her arms. "I just knew God healed me of that cancer!" she said. They found out later that the church didn't even believe in healing. God used her healing as a sign to those believers that He is still a miracle-working God. That cancer never came back.

Later a tumor appeared on Mom's thyroid. The doctors wanted to test it for cancer. Mom prayed the night before the test. "Lord, if I get weak and sick with this tumor, how am I going to help anybody?" With her lying on the table, the doctor held a needle in one hand and felt for the tumor with the other. Again he felt for the tumor. After a moment of silence, the doctor said, "Mrs. Yount, I can't do this test. I can't find the tumor. It's gone!"

Mom said, "I shimmied off the table and staggered down the hallway under the power of God like a drunkard. The Great Physician beat the doctors to it."

When in her 70s, Mom faced quadruple bypass surgery. I prayed for her the night before, and then she prayed for herself. Her prayer was so short it concerned me. She didn't even say "Amen." I wanted to tell her she should pray longer because of the seriousness of this surgery, but I didn't. I will never forget her short prayer that night. She prayed, "Lord, tomorrow morning is one of the reasons I've served You my whole life." That was it. She came through that surgery with flying colors. When she turned 80 years old, she was working in an assisted living home taking care of older people. She told us, "All these people are old in here."

A couple years later, her family doctor said, "From what we see this time, you will have to quit your job and stop driving your car."

He shouldn't have touched mom's car. With the doctor's report, Mom had quit her job and the state took her license. Mom called me one night and said, "Bill, my best friends are calling me to encourage me, but they end up reminding me of all my problems. I told them all, 'I don't have any problems. I just keep going.'"

The following Sunday she went to church to be anointed and prayed for by the elders. She called me that evening and said, "They anointed me with oil and prayed. I believe God healed me again, and I want my license back!"

Mom started calling up her doctors every other day demanding another test for her illness. She finally wore one doctor out. He gave her another test. As he read the test results with my mother sitting in his office, he stopped halfway through the report and looked at her: "Mrs. Yount, I think you can go back to work now."

Mom said, "How am I going to get there?"

The doctor said, "Let me see what I can do." This is unheard of at mom's age of 82 years old, but Mom got her license back and drove again.

Mom's Foot Totally Healed

When we get a breakthrough or victory, it's preparation for what is to come. Our family was shocked as the call came saying our mother had fallen down the basement steps and broken her ankle severely. Through surgery they put eleven pins and a plate in her ankle. From her battling with diabetes, the ankle refused to heal. The doctors finally said, "Mrs.

Capturing the Supernatural: Healed!

Yount, if the ankle does not begin to heal in a couple weeks, we are considering amputation." They marked mom's leg and explained about the artificial foot and said, "You'll get along fine with it."

But Mom prophesied to the doctors, "Whenever I go to heaven, I am taking my foot with me!"

Mom often told her doctors *who* was in the process of healing her, so that when it happened they knew they had very little to do with it. Weeks went by with no healing. The doctors told the family, "The foot is dead. It is black and has no circulation. You can take her anywhere else, but it's too late." If you have been given a "no hope" report from a doctor, I strongly recommend you get a second opinion.

The Lord led my mother to a doctor in Pittsburgh, Pennsylvania for a second opinion, and I went with her to see him. As he looked at Mom's foot, he said, "I'm going to try a couple things," and he walked out of the room. I followed him and asked what he really thought. He said, "I believe there's hope."

I never heard those words from any of her other doctors. His words encouraged the whole family. I stayed the following week for Mom's surgery. As the doctors came into her room that night to give her the report, the lead doctor said, "Mrs. Yount, I believe when you go to heaven, you will be taking your foot with you." This surgeon took the eleven pins and plate back out! After a battle of believing for five long months with special therapy, Mom's foot was totally healed.

She Kept Outliving Her Doctors and Diseases

At 88 years old, my mother was living in the assisted living home where she used to work years ago. She was battling some health problems, but she still got around well, went to church on Sundays, and lived to help others. One day she told the director, "I don't know why I am here in this place, for God has healed me so many times before."

The director's son spoke up and said, "Maybe God sent you here to tell us about Him."

Seldom would a day go by that I didn't call her on the phone. Why? I am still learning from her. I think that's why God extended her life for so long—for my sake and others. She had a cancerous tumor removed from her stomach recently and did well—no chemotherapy was needed. She kept outliving her doctors and diseases. Her wisdom outlasted her enemies and mine, too.

Once when I talked to Mom, she said, "Bill, I can't tell everyone this for they wouldn't believe it, but I wanted to let you know. I was feeling discouraged and all of a sudden I was in the lap of Jesus. I don't know how I got there. He put His arm around me and I felt the greatest peace I have ever known."

This is one more reason why I called Mom every day—to see what God was doing in her life. The day finally came when I called her and there was no answer, but her healings and miracles will continue to touch multitudes.

Bill Yount is a home missionary in his church, Bridge of Life in Hagerstown, Maryland. He is currently an advisor at large for Aglow International. Bill faithfully served in prison ministry for twenty-three years and now travels full time, both in the US and internationally, ministering in churches and Aglow circles. Humility and humor characterize his ministry as he brings forth a fresh word that is in season wherever he goes, proclaiming the word of the Lord! The *shofar*, a ram's horn, is often used in his meetings, breaking the powers of darkness over regions, churches, and households. His ministry is aptly called *Blowing the Shofar Ministries*. The *shofar* represents God's breath blowing into the nostrils of His people, reviving them and awakening the lost. Many of God's messages, which Bill ministers prophetically, come out of his everyday life with his family and friends. For more information, go to his website at: billyount.com.

Note from the publisher: Our condolences go out to the Yount family as they celebrate the homegoing of Bill's mother, who passed away at ninety years of age, shortly before this book was released.

CAPTURING THE SUPERNATURAL
Ordinary People, Extraordinary God

EMOTIONAL HEALING

Restoring the Shame

Mike Rizzo

Restoring the Shame

Mike Rizzo

The Heartache of Loss

She was an art therapist; I discovered that in our first session. While she didn't do a whole lot of praying or give me Scripture to study, she did however, give me art assignments, drawing out my thoughts and emotions, and then we'd talk for a while. I never dreamed as a thirty-nine year old pastor that cutting out pictures from magazines to make a collage could be an on-ramp for spiritual encounter.

"You're grieving," the therapist said. "You've experienced a loss in your life and this is why you're feeling the way you are." She was right. Not only was I grieving but I was being initiated by the Father into a deeper level of manhood and leadership. Looking back, it all makes sense. At the time, nothing made much sense.

We had been on pastoral staff of a church for ten years; it was my first "home church," and the pastor was a father figure to me. We felt fruitful, comfortable, and content. Our three children, ages eight, ten, and eleven, were integrated into the church family, had good friends, and we lived in a very nice home. None of us desired to move.

The whole process felt like a loss to me. My pastor was wise enough to know that I needed to spread my wings and leave my comfort zone. He was gracious to find me a small pastorate in a nearby city where I would be pruned into a greater fruitfulness. *God is kind to build a nest for us when we need it; and kind to release us when it's time.*

Capturing the Supernatural: Healed!

Much of this process was new to me, as I had never been mentored by elders growing up. We were a Catholic family, and I am grateful for some very meaningful traditions and solid creedal teaching, but I was largely unfathered. My dad was a hard worker and a good provider; both parents had giving hearts. Dad expressed himself through money and Mom through cooking.

The Absent Father

As teenagers my parents were marked by the hardships of the Great Depression, a decade that saw unemployment hit twenty-five percent in the United States and even higher in other countries. Mom and Dad personally experienced a global culture of "lack," hence their motivation to "work and save." Obviously not a bad financial practice, no matter the monetary climate, but for me this equated to an absent father.

How does all this relate to me ending up in art therapy as a thirty-nine-year-old pastor? Hopefully I can tie it all together. But first I need to share some background.

My best friend in my early years was a neighbor girl named Kim. We mainly played dolls. Yes, I was "Ken" and she was "Barbie." I distinctly remember her parents as well. Joe was the nicest guy, a distributor for a soda company, which meant a regular supply of free soda for our household. Jean was an attractive woman with a strong personality. I discerned even at the young age of five that she was the leader in the house.

> The heart and soul of a young boy and girl are hungry and thirsty for belonging and affirmation. No amount of money, food, or possessions can fill this vacuum.

Attending Catholic grade school, most of my teachers were nuns, interspersed with a few female "lay teachers" along the way. At home I was with Mom most of the time. In addition to his jobs, Dad was a volunteer at the local fire company. Sometimes he took me with him and I got to play on the fire trucks—by myself. Dad's place was at the bar, drinking with his friends. My reward: a bag of chips and a soda, and being introduced to the guys. Then it was back to playing—alone.

What sort of conclusion does a young boy come to in his mind when year after year his heart is left un-nurtured? "There is something wrong with me." Or, "I must not be enough." My dad never directly told me these things. The heart and soul of a young boy and girl are hungry and thirsty for belonging and affirmation. Thus the absence of these things sends a message. No amount of money, food, or possessions can fill this vacuum.

The Effects of Shame

As a wiser man today (but still learning) I can look in retrospect and see that I was being impacted by a primitive human emotion that everyone to some degree will experience—shame. It relayed to me the message, "Somehow I am flawed," and because I don't hear the other kids in school or on the playground sharing a similar heart story as mine, then I must be the only one who feels this way. How uniquely depressing!

Shame taught me that because I was flawed, I was unworthy of love and belonging. Because shame is what it is, it works hard to stay hidden. (Thanks to my art therapist for those collages. Seriously, they were a flotation device to help surface my heart.)

Okay, here's a few more dots to connect in my story. One of my antidotes for shame was to escape into fantasy. Yes, I had a social life in the neighborhood; I played sandlot baseball and football, but I spent lots of hours in front of our television set, mostly alone. Mom was in the house somewhere, sewing or cleaning or cooking. A fairly harmless activity—how bad could those shows have been back in the sixties? This is true compared to today. But for me, I learned how to live vicariously through others, which became a setup for later passivity in my life, confirming my inadequacy.

On a healthier note I was an avid reader. Our school had a mobile library that came to our parking lot every so often. I loved the smell of books and read great adventures about pioneers, cowboys, and sports heroes. By the way, I graduated from playing dolls with Kim and found a new best friend, a boy in my grade named Charlie. This was a wonderful reprieve for me. We were close for a couple of years, and I felt good about our friendship. Sadly, after we left grade school, we drifted apart.

Trying to Get Along with Dad

Meanwhile, I learned how to get along with my dad. First, avoidance; second, perfection. Mom had a nickname for dad; it was "Nerves." When we heard him pull in the driveway, we tensed up. Invariably he would find something "wrong" in the house. "Who left the light on downstairs?" "Where are my keys?" "Why is this door open?"

I remember once when I was washing our family car—a 1967 Ford Galaxy 500, a real beauty. A young boy in charge of a water hose—now that is empowering. It was fun to wash the car until the day Dad came home and observed how long I spent in the rinse cycle. "We're on a water meter, you know," he yelled. From then on I only washed the car when I knew for sure he would be gone for a while.

Multiple memories and interactions with Dad left me as a fearful boy in many respects. I did, however, give perfectionism my best shot. Perfectionism is the lie that if you do everything right, then you won't feel shame. (I didn't have the vocabulary for all these words at the time, but the concept was being branded into me.) Perfectionism is an addictive belief system with its primary focus on doing everything perfectly in order to avoid shame. "I will always be worthy if I please everyone all of the time."

When my grade school years were done, my tumultuous teen years began. I'm so grateful that we were Christian parents when raising our own teens. We refused to accept the dreary predictions that people warned us with: "Wait until they become teenagers." In my own case, however, I had no protection on my perimeter; my teen years were horrible.

I was the classic loner in school. I judged everyone around me. Those who are bound by shame tend to rejoice at the demise of those around

Restoring the Shame

Mike Rizzo

them. That's one reason why they say kids can be cruel; they are usually compensating for how they feel inside by finding someone worse off.

To be totally honest, later in my life I was still prone to rejoice when a pastor in my city was having problems in his church. This was a means of self-protection for my own fragile esteem. The proper response of compassion ("to suffer with") was sorely lacking in me. *Shame tends to drain the inner resources leaving little to spare for others.*

In high school I hated jocks and cheerleaders, classmates with straight As, and anyone else I was jealous of—for whatever reason. Self-loathing made "me" almost impossible to live with at times—for myself that is. The subsequent anger and frustration that built up inside needed targets to fire on, so I pulled people down in my mind.

Coming to Christ

The labyrinth of emotions and thoughts at my core was massively rocked when I gave my life to Christ at age twenty-one. At this writing I am celebrating forty years of being a new man. I did a one-eighty; my parents were astounded, as was my brother. I led them both to Christ within three years; my dad was influenced at a slower pace, but he eventually came around.

My mom started to show symptoms of Alzheimer's in 1991, and until her death in 1999 my dad cared for her. He kept her at home; we helped when we could but it was pretty much all him, serving my mom, taking care of all her needs. It was in this time frame that I began my transition season of pastoring my own church.

While I felt proficient at the home church, under the covering of my senior pastor and surrounded by a large staff, I felt unequipped, weak, and inadequate as the new pastor of my own church. (The shame triggers were in abundance.)

So why would my pastor of eighteen years, with whom I'd served on staff for ten of those, suggest that it was time for me to step out on my own? *My soul felt the familiar tremor: there is something wrong with you; you are not good enough.* Most women experience shame in the area of

Capturing the Supernatural: Healed!

appearance: "How do I look?" Most men are triggered by the perception of weakness: "Am I viewed as successful, adequate, and strong?"

Closing the Church Doors

Looking back, it was a wonderfully fruitful time. Highlight films are fun to watch; one gets to select the best. There were ups and downs for sure. But after ten years of leading this church we closed its doors. We were seventy people at our peak; at the end, maybe twenty.

When we first began the pastorate I felt that I heard a word from the Lord: "I've sent you here to bring this season to a proper ending, to give this church a proper burial." Wow! Would God say something like that? The church was begun in 1926. Was it really my assignment to take it down the home stretch? How could that possibly be success?

Yet I was in it to win it. I only shared this word with my wife, and I think she actually forgot about it as the years progressed. I loved our congregation. I remember saying to them, "I plan to be here to officiate the weddings of your children." And I sincerely meant it.

Closing the church was a necessity. At the time I was becoming emotionally worn and at the end of my rope. Incidentally, the church remained closed for a year or two and was then reopened with a new pastor. It remains a functioning church today. Though low in attendance, we left the church with no mortgage, a paid off parsonage, and a few grand in the bank—God's favor. The field was plowed under and a new field later planted.

Imagine the potential remorse and shame that might come over closing down a church. Yes, there was a battle, but I was amazed at how strong God was in my weakness. My wife and I took regular jobs in the marketplace and discovered that we still had our identity in Christ outside of formal ministry. This was the year in which my dad developed heart problems.

Roles Reversed

He had a stroke and lived his final two years in a nursing home. I was the power of attorney for my dad. During this season, my boyhood role was reversed; I was now the caretaker. When he couldn't use his arms, I held the coffee cup to his lips to drink and feed him his "French crueler." I wheeled him around the facility and occasionally took him out for a ride. I watched my dad serve my mom in the most humble way possible. She was unable to give anything in return. I was able to serve him in a similar way during those final two years.

As Dad's condition worsened, I was cleaning out the family home in preparation to sell. It was the only house I had ever known. They bought it in 1956; we moved there when I was two. In the course of trying to throw out or give away years of accumulated stuff, I relived many a memory. It was one of the most wonderful times of closure I've ever had. I wept on a few occasions in the basement of our house, a place where I spent hours in play as a child.

And then came the frosting on the cake: at the graveside, the two marines folded the flag that had draped Dad's coffin. "On behalf of the President of the United States, the Commandant of the Marine Corps, and a grateful nation, please accept this flag as a symbol of our appreciation for your loved one's service to country and corps." I've got two Marines in front of me. I'm being handed a flag. And I'm being reminded that my dad served his nation in a war. I felt a manly pride in being the son of this man.

Goodbye Shame

Emotionally it felt like I was moving at "warp speed"—grieving the loss but also sensing something being built within me that I never had before. It was my initiation into manly growth, a quality that had never been bestowed upon me as a young boy.

> Emotionally it felt like I was moving at "warp speed"—grieving the loss but also sensing something being built within me that I never had before.

I have found that "restoration" is not an itemized exchange. What I mean is that it's not some kind of orderly, chronological process that you go through year by year to heal all of your wounds with Mom or Dad and then

Capturing the Supernatural: Healed!

become complete as a man or woman. I have found it to be very seasonal, many times unexpected, and many times very messy on the front end.

Getting married is huge. Having children is huge. Dealing with the death of a parent is huge. Any major transition is a portal. Some call them rites of passage. They are transitional seasons. Basic rule of thumb: *Make the most of them when they come.*

When I left my home church at the age of thirty-nine to be initiated into a new season of my manhood I was given a prophetic word: "You were a son in the house; now you are a father in the house." When I left that graveside at the age of fifty-two I sensed the passing of another baton. I was the father now.

Shame is a distant memory today. When it tries to visit, our meeting is brief, and thankfully, we've grown distant. I have cherished memories of my Dad. I am so thankful for my first spiritual father who poured into my life for eighteen years and launched me into my first pastorate. My journey mate and covenant marriage partner of thirty-four years is faithfully by my side. I will most likely never visit an art therapist again, but God had Sandy in the right place at the right time.

Every step is a valuable one on this supernatural journey.

Mike and Anne Rizzo were born and raised in Buffalo, New York and committed their lives to Christ as young adults in 1975. They were married in 1981 and have served in pastoral ministry for over thirty years. In 2007 they relocated to Kansas City, Missouri to be full-time intercessory prayer missionaries at the International House of Prayer, where they serve as directors of marriage and family ministries. Mike and Anne carry a passion for personal mentoring, teaching, and raising up marriages that exalt the name of Jesus. They released their first book, *Longing for Eden: Embracing God's Vision in Your Marriage,* in 2012. For more information, visit their website and blog at: marriagelongingforeden.com.

Making Room for the Supernatural

Hermie Reynolds

Making Room for the Supernatural

Hermie Reynolds

Stirring Faith

As a child growing up in South Africa I loved to play in the vegetable garden, lying in the dirt, daydreaming about fairies. After I was done playing I always went back inside the house and told my mom about the fairies I saw amongst the flowers on the beanstalks. To me, that was supernatural! Somehow we all long to connect with a supernatural reality outside of ourselves. We know we're not alone, but if no one has taught us about God it is hard to find Him. I grew up in a Christian home and I heard the Bible stories of how God helped people in miraculous ways. In the children's Bible I saw pictures of people who dressed so differently than we do that those stories felt far removed from my life. I assumed that God worked during that time, but He was not doing anything today. In the Bible I read about many people who were healed by Jesus, but growing up there was no expectation that God could heal. I never saw Him heal anyone in answer to prayer. The answer might come through a doctor who helped the person get well, but we never experienced or heard of any miracles.

God felt like a distant grandfather, and I wasn't sure whether He had time for me or even if He liked me. The thought didn't even cross my mind that He desired to have a relationship with me and wanted to be involved in my life. I didn't experience Him; He felt absent in my life. When my Father was terminally ill, my mother had an experience in which she saw Jesus and the angel of death standing in the bedroom

CAPTURING THE SUPERNATURAL: HEALED!

door and Jesus said, "It is not yet time." Our Christian background didn't make room for any supernatural experiences, so she told no one about it. My mom shared this with me many years later when I told her about how God was moving in my life. Until I was twenty years old I went to church and obeyed rules, but I did not experience power in my religion and had no relationship with God.

When I found Jesus, my search ended and the journey began. I had attended church for many, many years, but never realized I had to make my faith personal. I had to come to the decision to receive Jesus as the Lord of my life. Suddenly my life had more joy and purpose. God saw my hungry heart, but He also knew the walls of tradition and religion that I been brought up to believe in needed to be torn down gradually. A friend who attended a different church, who was more open to the working of the Holy Spirit, invited me to a Bible study. Every time she invited me I declined because I was a little bit fearful of the unknown. But the Holy Spirit was patient with me. He came again and again and spoke through people or books to draw me in the direction that God wanted me to go.

When our firstborn was eighteen months old, she was hospitalized for two to three days due to dehydration. During that time a lady from a church visited the sick in the hospital and asked permission to pray for my daughter. I agreed. This lady prayed for our daughter's healing. In her prayer she prayed that God would receive the honor for her healing. I was a bit surprised by this prayer, because I had no expectation that God would heal her and had never before given God the credit for healing anyone. The next day my daughter was well and we went home. The Holy Spirit used this prayer to stir my heart to think about the possibility that God could still heal.

Truth of the Word

Six months later we moved to a different city. God saw the hunger in my heart, and He sent another lady across my path. She invited me to a weekly interdenominational Bible study where women from different churches gathered. They had just started a study about the Holy Spirit. It

Making Room for the Supernatural

was an amazing time for me to see the Scriptures in the Bible about the Holy Spirit. I was very hungry to learn more about God, and there was something different about this group. The Bible came alive to me and it felt like I had a spiritual meal after I had been there. I felt spiritually satisfied when I went home.

The leader of the group invited a traveling guest speaker to come and minister for a weekend. This lady was a powerful Bible teacher and I soaked up the teaching like a sponge. I couldn't get enough. Over the next year I ordered many of her messages. It opened a whole new world to me as I learned more about the Holy Spirit and the power in speaking the Word and healing. I started to see that God is the one *"Who forgives all your iniquities, who heals all your diseases"* (Psalm 103:3 NKJV). The Old Testament prophesied that Jesus would die that we can be healed (see Isaiah 53:5), and it is written in the New Testament too, *"He personally carried our sins in his body on the cross so that we can be dead to sin and live for what is right. By his wounds you are healed"* (1 Peter 2:24 NLT). The truth of the Word opened my eyes to the fact that God can heal me, that we are actually already healed at the cross, and that we just need to apply what Jesus has done in our lives. Healing doesn't depend on whether we are good enough. In the same way that Jesus died for our sins and we receive the gift of salvation, we can receive healing. This puts healing on a whole different foundation.

As I soaked up all this Bible teaching, my faith and belief in God was strengthened and I grew spiritually by leaps and bounds. I learned that the Word of God has power when we speak a Scripture mixed with faith in the authority of the Holy Spirit. The time came when I had to put in practice what I had learned. One Saturday morning I woke up feeling sick to my stomach. I knew that I had to apply what I had been learning. I prayed and spoke the Word as I lay in bed. I didn't get well immediately but kept going in faith, and within four hours I felt much better and got up. I knew this was a twenty-four hour bug, but the medicine of the Word worked faster than twenty-four hours.

Do we really know the power that is available to us when we tap into God's authority? *"What is the exceeding greatness of His power*

CAPTURING THE SUPERNATURAL: HEALED!

toward us who believe, according to the working of His mighty power which He worked in Christ when He raised Him from the dead and seated Him at His right hand in the heavenly places" (Ephesians 1:19-20 NKJV). If we know the power that can be released through faith in God and the power of the Holy Spirit, we will not be in awe of any counterfeit power.

Do we really know the power in the name of Jesus? God has given Jesus the name with the highest authority in the universe. *"He (Jesus) humbled Himself and became obedient to the point of death, even the death of the cross. Therefore God also has highly exalted Him and given Him the name which is above every name"* (Philippians 2:8-9 NKJV). If you continue to read this Scripture in the Bible you will find that every knee in heaven, on earth, and under the earth will bow before Jesus, whether in this life or one day when the person stands before God. When we use the name of Jesus with the honor and respect that it deserves in faith that what God said is true, the Holy Spirit power is released and situations change.

I am thankful for my foundational years in the Word, because they taught me to stand on the truth of the Bible and not on how I felt and what I saw. I learned that the Word has greater authority than the natural. I also learned that when the Holy Spirit is highlighting a Scripture and I speak it forth, something happens in the spirit realm and breakthrough comes. So that's what I do. I declare what He gives me day after day until there is a breakthrough. In medieval times, armies broke down the door of the castle or wall with a battering ram, and declaring Scripture works the same way. It breaks through the resistance in the spirit. Daniel prayed and twenty-one days later his prayer was answered. God heard him right at the beginning, but the angel who delivered the answer was held up in the heavens by the demonic ruler in the spirit realm over Persia (see Daniel 10:13). God miraculously brought the Israelites out of Egypt, but when they came to Canaan they had to follow Holy Spirit-directed orders and fight to get the land God promised to them. When we have the Word, the Holy Spirit, and faith, we will see God move in wonderful ways.

Making Room for the Supernatural

Faith of a Child

When our children were young, we prayed with them for healing when they were sick or got hurt. Our youngest sons were about third and fourth grade when one of them sprained their ankle. They shared a room, so when I put them to bed, his brother and I prayed for the hurt ankle. When I finished praying, the brother said he saw an angel come down and work on his brother's ankle. The next morning when our son woke up, the ankle was fully healed!

> When I finished praying, the brother said he saw an angel come down and work on his brother's ankle. The next morning when our son woke up, the ankle was fully healed!

God must have sent an angel that night. God can heal in so many ways. We just need to be obedient and open to listen to His Spirit.

I learned about healing when our kids were little. For them it was natural to say, "Mom, can you pray for me?" Three of our kids played sports in high school, and over the years they had several injuries, sprained ankles, and hurt shoulders. When our youngest was a senior in high school he got hurt a couple of times. I was so blessed that he would still ask me to pray for him. With basketball injuries I often had to pray more than once. It might be better the next day, but not completely healed. When we take medicine for an illness, we take it once a day or twice and sometimes three times a day. I pray for a situation again and again if I don't see complete healing the first time. Usually I prayed in the evening and maybe again in the morning. My son would go about his business and go to practice, and many times life would go on and we would forget he had the problem.

Our oldest son played basketball too. When he was a senior in high school, he was playing in a game. At one point he went in for a rebound and rolled his ankle. It was very swollen and he couldn't put any weight on it. He had to use crutches. There was a healing evangelist in town and our family went to the meeting that weekend. The man prayed for our son, and he began to walk on the injured foot right away. It still hurt a little but he could do it. On Monday I took our son to the doctor and they

Capturing the Supernatural: Healed!

took x-rays of the foot. The doctor was surprised that the swelling was gone. The trainer who had looked at his foot Friday evening was from that sports medicine office and had told the doctor about the injury. The doctor looked at the x-rays and said that he could only see an old injury that was healed on the bone. Our son never had an injury to that foot before that, so what he was seeing was God's healing power that had touched my son! The doctor said to give it a rest for a few days and then he could start practicing again. Within a week he was back at practice. It was an amazing recovery; our daughter had rolled her ankle playing basketball two years before this happened and it had taken four to six weeks to heal. I was so thankful that God healed our son so he could play basketball in his senior year.

One of our sons who is in Bible school helped with a teen summer camp in 2014. He saw a boy from his group sitting in the church auditorium while the other kids were playing dodgeball in the gym. He asked him why he wasn't playing with them and the boy said that he'd hurt his back a few months ago. He had had a bad fall and was no longer able to play. My son prayed for him. The next day he saw the boy running around and stopped him and asked him, "Dude, how's your back?" The boy answered that his back was fine. It was then that my son realized that God had healed this boy!

Emotional Healing

The biggest miracle of healing in my life was in the area of my emotions. My dad was absent emotionally, away from home for long hours, and this left a huge gap in my life. In my late twenties the Holy Spirit began the process of emotional healing in me. At some point while growing up, without even realizing that I had done it, I had decided to shut down my emotions to block out the pain in my heart.

One day as I was walking in a bookstore I saw a stained glass ornament with John 15:13 on it: *"Greater love has no one than this, than to lay down one's life for his friends"* (NKJV). When I read it, I suddenly realized that I didn't believe that Jesus loved me. I looked at the Scripture again and said to myself, *What more can Jesus do for you?*

Making Room for the Supernatural

He died for you? There is nothing more anyone can do than to give their life and die for someone. The Holy Spirit used this simple ornament to reveal to me that there was a problem with my emotions. I realized that at times I couldn't feel hurt or joy, just a void. I had built a hard shell around my heart, protecting me from the pain of rejection that I felt from my dad. The problem was it didn't just keep the bad feelings out, but it also hindered me from experiencing good feelings like joy. The Holy Spirit worked little by little. He uncovered one thing at a time and brought healing to my life.

My next Holy Spirit appointment was when a traveling missionary came into town and he talked about the Father heart of God. I cried my eyes out. I didn't even know why I was crying or what was going on inside me. Just hearing that God has the heart of a daddy touched me deeply. Soon after that I signed up for a training seminar at church. One of the sessions was about rejection. I didn't think I had a problem in that area until the Holy Spirit showed me how much of a perfectionist I was. If I made the slightest mistake I mercilessly judged and condemned myself. I wondered where this rejection came from. An opportunity to receive some training came that brought more answers. Iniquities can be passed down from generation to generation (see Exodus 20:5). I realized I was probably under some generational rejection, but that was not the only place it was coming from. The teacher explained that it is easier for a child who was abused to know that he or she has to forgive their father, but more difficult for someone to see the damage an absent father has done in their heart. That's when I knew the origin of my rejection. My dad had worked in the daytime and most evenings too. I felt that I couldn't be mad at him for working hard for our family, but when I heard this lady speak, I knew that deep down in my heart there must be hurt and rejection because my dad had had so little time for me. Now that the wound was opened up, the Holy Spirit could do an even deeper healing.

Bit by bit it all unfolded. My mom told me that my father never wanted to have children. He was the oldest of twelve children and the youngest was born when he was eighteen. Because of this, he didn't like

Capturing the Supernatural: Healed!

babies and never wanted to be around them. I was the first child to be born in our family. It wasn't that my dad didn't like me or didn't want me specifically; it came from his past history. This manifested in my life in my low self-esteem and how I overcommitted myself because I didn't have proper boundaries. I struggled with depression from time to time as well. This was all covered up by being a busy mom of four young children, leading the children's ministry at our church with my husband who worked full time. I did all the curriculum planning and scheduling for this ministry. On top of that, my personality type thrives when I am busy. It wasn't awful, but I didn't allow myself to rest and I said yes to too many things. I was a Martha on the outside with a Mary yearning for more intimate time with Jesus on the inside.

How wonderful it is that God knows us! He knew exactly what the next step should be to bring me into greater emotional healing and wholeness. A lady at church told me about a book that had made a strong impact on her life. I bought the book and saw the importance of the role of a father in a child's life. I did not remember actually judging my dad for not being there for me, but seeing the fruit of that in my life, I realized I must have made judgments. In fact, my husband worked most evenings, just like my dad had. In faith I repented of my judgments against my father—that he wasn't there for me, he wasn't involved in my life, it didn't feel like he loved me, etc. My husband went out to see a client that day. When he came back I felt a great deal better than I had before; walls that often went up between us came down that day. My relationship with my husband improved a lot and I began to see God more as a father. When my judgments against my dad were still in place it felt like God was in church on Sundays but He was absent during the week. Now I could sense His involvement in my life all the time.

A Depressed Christian?

All my problems weren't gone, however; I still struggled with an odd three-day bout of depression that just hit me sometimes. When it happened, I felt like there were bricks attached to my arms and it was difficult to perform even my everyday tasks. I was a born-again,

Making Room for the Supernatural

> I was a born-again, Spirit-filled Christian, so I couldn't understand how I could be struggling like this.

I was a born-again, Spirit-filled Christian, so I couldn't understand how I could be struggling like this. I should be happy that Jesus saved me, gave me purpose for life, and that His Holy Spirit lived inside me. Yet, I struggled. My depression usually came after I experienced disappointment. This depression would always last for three days and then lift. I found another book where I learned how babies can be affected by trauma they experience in the womb. As I was reading the end of a chapter, I suddenly had this odd sensation in my spirit; it felt like there was rope tied around my feet and I was drowning. It only lasted for a few seconds, and then it was gone. *What was that?* The next day I walked past the television and there was a picture of a girl swimming in the ocean amongst seaweed. As I saw it, an intense fear gripped me! *What was going on?* I decided to ask one of the pastor's wives if she could pray with me.

Around that same time my mom told me that I had been stuck in her womb for three days. When my mother went into labor, her water broke on a Friday evening. My dad took her to the hospital, but the doctor was out of town that weekend. Her contractions eventually subsided, and she spent the weekend in the hospital. The doctor returned Monday, and Tuesday morning they induced labor. My mother said that I was stuck in the birth canal for three days. The sensation that I had of a rope tied around my feet must have been how I had felt. While the pastor's wife was praying for me, I saw myself stuck in a pipe. My arms were in a downward position—the same position a baby experiences in birth. As she continued to pray, I saw Jesus lift me out of that pipe. The Holy Spirit brought to my mind that during this time I probably made a vow in my spirit, something like, *"If this is life, then life stinks and I don't want to live."* From then on, every time I faced a disappointment, this vow triggered and plunged me into despair and depression. This was what I was experiencing. When the vow was broken, that cycle stopped. If the Holy Spirit hadn't revealed this to me I probably would still struggle with depression. Medication wouldn't have helped because the problem was in my spirit.

Capturing the Supernatural: Healed!

A merry heart makes a cheerful countenance, but by sorrow of the heart the spirit is broken (Proverbs 15:13 NKJV).

That prayer time brought big breakthrough for overcoming the depression that had plagued me for so long. Understanding the root of the problem and receiving prayer brought the breakthrough. In the twenty years since that time I have not had even one bout of depression! I can handle disappointment a lot better, and it has made life much easier for me. Psalm 40 is a picture of what God has done for me: *"I waited patiently for the Lord to help me, and he turned to me and heard my cry. He lifted me out of the pit of despair, out of the mud and the mire. He set my feet on solid ground and steadied me as I walked along. He has given me a new song to sing, a hymn of praise to our God"* (Psalms 40:1-3 NLT).

America: Land of the Free and Home of the Brave

In 1999 we moved from South Africa to the United States. A whole new life awaited our family. Each member of our family responded differently to the change. We process things differently and have different personalities. Most of our children welcomed the move or were able to adjust to it quickly. My mom had such tenacity that no adversity could keep her down for long.

At our new church, I attended a class about boundaries. During this class the Holy Spirit showed me walls representing those boundaries. Instead of standing behind the wall looking out, I was sitting, hiding behind the wall. As I thought about this vision I realized that at certain times I used boundaries to hide so people couldn't come close to me. Then at other times I was such a people pleaser that I couldn't say no and ended up over committing myself and becoming overwhelmed. The Bible tells us, *"And you shall know the truth, and the truth shall make you free"* (John 8:32 NKJV). This truth brought a greater balance to my life.

God was not finished with me yet; another training course was slated for me. This time my husband went with me as well. Little did I know, God was peeling another layer of the onion back and bringing

Making Room for the Supernatural

more truth that would bring me to a new level of freedom. The training dealt with how lies can get stuck in our minds during traumatic events, or when we are wounded or hurt, especially during childhood. We cannot process what happens to us as a child objectively, so the beliefs that get ingrained in our minds are often wrong, especially in a situation when a person is hurt by other people or traumatized. I realized I probably had many lies stuck in my mind, lies about my self-image and performance. When our instructor asked for a volunteer I put my hand up. She prayed with me and I felt a burning sensation on my arms. It was a bodily sensation that I was feeling connected to when I had been burned by boiling water when I was a year old. The lady prayed and asked Jesus what He wanted to show me about this. I saw a picture of myself sitting in a big hand. I felt comforted that God held me in the palm of His hand even in the midst of this traumatic experience. He took care of me. Seeing this vision brought peace into that traumatic event. Suddenly, I knew that God took care of me. This helped me to be able to come to rest in God's love and be able to trust the fact that He will continue to take care of me.

I spent hours reading through the manual for the class. As I read some of the testimonies of wrong beliefs or lies that people had, I was stirred to ask the Holy Spirit to speak to me and bring truth. I could feel that I was coming into greater freedom. The truth was setting me free!

We live in a day where there are many kids who grow up without dads or have dads who work long hours. There are many children who need emotional healing. Many are addicted to different things; some cut themselves, are sexually immoral, have eating disorders, or a host of other problems, but what they really need to know is that Jesus cared enough about them to die for them and that they are truly loved by Jesus and their heavenly Daddy. They need to know in their hearts that nothing they can do or could have done is so terrible that God would not receive them. They need to know that the sacrifice of Jesus is enough to help anyone. It starts with turning to Jesus and receiving what He has done on the cross. The woman with the issue of blood told herself that if she could only touch the hem of Jesus' garment, she would be made

CAPTURING THE SUPERNATURAL: HEALED!

whole, or healed (see Matthew 9:21). The word "whole" is the Greek word *sozo* which means "to save a suffering one (from perishing), i.e. one suffering from disease, to make well, heal, restore to health."[1] Jesus came to make us well—body, soul, and spirit.

God Is Good All the Time

Looking back, I can see how good God has been to us. Around 2009 my husband had trouble with his knee. If he bent his knee and turned it a certain way, it would come out of place and lock painfully so that he couldn't straighten it. He visited the doctor and an MRI showed that he had a torn meniscus that could only be repaired through surgery. During this time another missionary came to town; we went to hear him speak at someone's house. At the end of his talk, he asked if anyone needed prayer for healing, and my husband asked for prayer. The group laid hands on him and prayed for him. He didn't feel anything specific, but since he received prayer for his knee he has been playing tennis, exercises regularly, and laid hardwood floors without his knee giving him any problems! I am so thankful that we serve a God who can help us and heal us.

Admittedly, there are some areas where I haven't seen healing and have not experienced a breakthrough, but I found that some of these problems were caused by my diet. For instance, I found that the migraines I had were caused by preservatives in food. When I asked a doctor about it, he said my body was telling me that they were bad for me. He told me that I should be glad my body reacted as it did. Because most people don't show a reaction, even though the preservatives are bad for them they continue using them. My high blood pressure also came down when I made dietary changes. God gave us the responsibility to make good and wise choices, and He does not take it away. He wants us to take care of the body, the temple, He gave us!

---

1. Thayer and Smith. "Greek Lexicon entry for sozo." The KJV New Testament Greek Lexicon, accessed Masrch 16, 2015, http://www.biblestudytools.com/lexicons/greek/kjv/sozo.html.

Making Room for the Supernatural

Or do you not know that your body is the temple of the Holy Spirit who is in you, whom you have from God, and you are not your own? (1 Corinthians 6:19 NKJV)

In 2002 I went to a conference where a man who was a healing evangelist ministered. He asked the graduates of 1979 to stand and released over them a healing anointing. After that conference I saw some people healed or their health improved after I prayed for them. As I pray with people in the area of emotional healing I can tell when we hit the exact right spot. For example, when we find the lie they believe, the Holy Spirit brings truth quickly most of the time. This has convinced me that God is more eager to help us than we think He is. When I pray for healing, I pray as specifically as I am able. I command a muscle to be healed or a certain sickness to leave. In Scripture, Jesus spoke and the person was healed. In the same way, I speak by faith in authority of the name of Jesus to release the power of the Holy Spirit.

> In Scripture, Jesus spoke and the person was healed. In the same way, I speak by faith in authority of the name of Jesus to release the power of the Holy Spirit.

A few years ago I received a group text asking for prayer for a friend who had gone to the emergency room with chest pain; they said he was having a heart attack. We began praying. The next day test results showed that nothing was wrong! This man was thirty-nine years old at the time. Several of the men in his family had had heart attacks at age thirty-nine; this gave me the idea that there could be a generational curse at work. A week after this incident, a group from church gathered to pray for him. In faith I broke a curse on the family bloodline and took authority over a demonic spirit attached to it, commanding it to leave. My son was there and said that when I prayed he saw a demonic spirit leave and that the spirit had the same name as the man's last name. This man hasn't had a problem since. Not all sicknesses are demonic, but some can be influenced by demonic spirits.

When my sons were in fifth grade they played in a recreational soccer league. Usually kids don't get hurt in those leagues, but that year one kid

CAPTURING THE SUPERNATURAL: HEALED!

after another on the team kept getting hurt. Our son's friend broke his toe, then one of our sons rode his bike into a truck in the neighborhood and he could hardly walk. It didn't look like he had broken anything, but the bike handles hit him hard in his hips. It was already evening when it happened. We prayed for him when we put him in bed and the next morning he woke up and was fine. A few days later our other son, who was on the same team, got kicked in the knee. It was very swollen and he had to use crutches for a while. We prayed for him several times, but it didn't seem to help. A week later he went with me to a prayer group. At the end of the meeting, the ladies prayed for him. One lady had a word of knowledge that a boy on the team was saying that he wished certain kids would get hurt. She said that the words were working like a curse, and this was the reason so many kids on the team had been injured. They prayed for him and he got better very quickly. We have authority to break curses in the name of Jesus. I am thankful that we have the Holy Spirit who can give us revelation about such situations.

Healing Flows

In 2013 I hurt my arm. When I picked up my heavy book bag, a sharp pain went through my arm. It didn't feel like a muscle pain, or like I'd broken a bone, so I thought I would just take it slow for a few days and not pick up anything heavy with that arm. After a few days it felt better and I forgot about it. Later, I picked up the bag again and felt the same pain, so I gave my arm rest again. This continued for more than a month. Then a lady with a healing ministry came to town and I went to the meeting, hoping that I could receive prayer. When I got to the meeting it was crowded, and the only place I could sit was in the overflow room across the hallway. I figured there was very little chance I would receive prayer that night. The way this lady normally ministered was that after about an hour of worship, she called out different illnesses or health problems that the Holy Spirit showed her God wanted to heal that night. I decided that because God's presence was already there, I was just going to lean into it and lay hands on myself. I put my hand on my arm and released God's healing presence into my arm. I did that for half an hour or more while the worship was going on and different

Making Room for the Supernatural

sicknesses were being called out for healing. At the end of the evening I was feeling less pain in the arm and by the next day the pain was gone! My arm was fine and hasn't hurt since. Sometimes you don't need a minister to recognize your ailment to receive a touch from God. He already knows what you need!

> Sometimes you don't need a minister to recognize your ailment to receive a touch from God. He already knows what you need!

In June 2014 I hurt the plantar fasciitis muscle under my right foot. I did what I could do about it, resting it and hoping it would get better, but I just couldn't get it to be totally healed. After three months of struggling with this, I asked for prayer one morning at our House of Prayer meeting. They prayed for me and God healed that muscle. A few weeks later I injured the Achilles tendon on the other foot. It was a worse injury than the plantar fasciitis. I did what I could again—iced it and rested it. It felt better after a week and I went to the grocery store. After shopping, the injury was a lot worse. After another week of resting it was much better again, but there was still some pain that didn't want to subside. The whole time I had been thinking that it was nearly healed, and that I did not need to press in through prayer to get this foot completely healed. One morning as I was sitting at the House of Prayer I realized that we would soon be flying to South Africa and I would have to walk long distances in airports. I would really need to be able to walk without pain. I grabbed the bottle of anointing oil and anointed my heel, releasing healing into it. The pain completely left! The next day there was just a little bit of pain, so I anointed it and prayed again. My foot felt much better than it had in a long time.

Another time a man came into town who ushers in the presence of God through worship. He normally worships for at least an hour and a half until the presence of God fills the room, and then he calls out what he senses God wants to heal. The day before this meeting, my husband's knee had suddenly swelled up about an inch with water on his knee. He was standing in the back of the meeting, just observing. This was not the typical church service. He didn't receive prayer and nobody laid hands

Capturing the Supernatural: Healed!

on him, but by the next day the swelling was all gone! Just being in that atmosphere of the presence of God brought healing.

In 2007 I had a dream about a healing evangelist who prayed for me. In the dream, as the person prayed the Holy Spirit picked me up, turned me upside down, and stuck my feet on the ceiling. I realized that is what God has done to my thinking. In the past I didn't believe in healing, and God has turned that mentality upside down. Now I believe that God heals. God is going to turn many people upside down. People who don't or didn't believe in healing will completely change what they believe as the Holy Spirit teaches them.

Message from God

Then, after doing all those things, I will pour out my Spirit upon all people. Your sons and daughters will prophesy. Your old men will dream dreams, and your young men will see visions. In those days I will pour out my Spirit even on servants—men and women alike (Joel 2:28-29 NLT).

One afternoon in 2003 I lay down to rest for a few minutes. As I was almost asleep, I saw an image of someone pushing a white envelope under the door. It felt so real that I was startled and woke up. I even went to the door and looked to see if I could find the envelope but there was nothing. I realized I must have seen or experienced this in my spirit, and in that envelope there must be a message from God. I wondered what the message was. I decided to get my journal and ask the Holy Spirit to share the message with me. This is what I have written down:

My dear child,

You are invited to join Joel's army. It is an army of radical, committed warriors. The requirement for this army is that you serve the Lord your God with all your heart, mind, and soul. He will accomplish that in you, if you are willing.

Are you willing?

Love,

Making Room for the Supernatural

Your Dad, Almighty God

Later that evening I checked my e-mail and there was a message about the commissioning of Joel's army. Joel's army refers to a people who will walk in the supernatural. In the book of Acts after the Holy Spirit was poured out, Peter quoted Joel 2:28-29 when the bystanders asked him what was going on (see Acts 2:17-20). If you look at the time this passage refers to, Peter said, *"In the last days"* and *"before that great and glorious day of the Lord arrives"* (Acts 2:17, 20).

In the book of Acts we read that the apostles and the church experienced miracles, prophecy, the Holy Spirit speaking to them, tongues, etc. Then it was like a death took place in the church in the dark ages and religion took over. A relationship with Jesus became a form or tradition. The Holy Spirit has been restoring the church to become like the church in the book of Acts again, a church that will walk in signs, wonders, and miracles.

One night I had a dream that a man who walked in a tremendous healing ministry prayed a release of signs, wonders, and miracles over a pastor. In the dream this man was preaching from 1 Thessalonians 5, and I had the perception that this was connected to Acts 29. Now Acts doesn't have a chapter 29. I have heard people say that Acts 29 still needs to be written. The believers who are walking in signs, wonders, and miracles on earth today are writing Acts 29 through their actions. In my Bible the heading with 1 Thessalonians 5 sums the chapter up by saying, "No one knows when the return of the Lord is." I believe this dream refers to an outpouring of God's Spirit in the last days with signs, wonders, and miracles. We don't know the exact time of the return of Jesus, but if you listen to and read what those who study the end times say, the return of Jesus is not far off. God desires to pour out His Spirit on all people so there will be many people who will walk like Jesus did, having compassion on the sick, pouring out the love of Jesus on hurt and broken people to give them hope. People do not only need physical healing; they are hurt, broken, and wounded in so many ways. Hurt and broken people hurt others. We can stop that cycle through the cross.

Capturing the Supernatural: Healed!

Jesus is the only one who can make us whole. He is the only one who can change our hearts to love others like He does.

Joel 2 Invitation

If you are reading this, God is extending this Joel 2 invitation to you. He wants people to walk in complete obedience to Him, hearing His voice, and following His Holy Spirit just like Jesus did. God will accomplish great exploits through these ones. They will be humble, not lovers of self, but lovers of the King. He is inviting you to live and walk in the most exciting relationship you will ever have. His Holy Spirit lives in you and you can experience the supernatural in your life. What will your answer be? Will you say yes to Him? He has much more in store for you—more than you can ever dream or imagine!

Hermie Reynolds is the author of *Discovering God* and *Discovering Jesus*, books that lead people into having a better understanding of God the Father and God the Son. Hermie and her husband, John, led the children's ministry at their church in South Africa for ten years. The family moved to Cincinnati in 1999, and she continues to be involved with teaching, helping with prayer ministry at church, as well as intercession at the Cincinnati House of Prayer. Hermie and John are part of the leadership team at the Oxford Vineyard Church where she is the pastor of discipleship. They have four grown children. Find out more about Hermie at www.discoveringgod.info.

CAPTURING THE SUPERNATURAL
Ordinary People, Extraordinary God

HEALING ANOINTING

Prayer in the Cave

John Burton

PRAYER IN THE CAVE
John Burton

There's Fire on Your Hand!

Often when I travel to various churches and conferences to minister, people tell me they see or sense fire on my right hand. I'll admit, it was strange the first time someone asked me if I could release the fire they saw burning on my hand into them. I glanced down at my five fingers and my palm and didn't see anything remarkable whatsoever. It was an average looking hand. Not even big enough to confidently palm a basketball. Of course, I did as she requested. I placed my hand on her shoulder and prayed that she would be filled with the fire of the Holy Spirit. That scenario has become a regular occurrence for me.

Several years prior I was leading a ministry in Manitou Springs, Colorado called Revolution House of Prayer. Some people consider Manitou Springs the most demonic region in the nation. It sits at the base of Pike's Peak and has been steeped in witchcraft and the occult for decades. While involved in that unusual town we experienced some dramatic encounters both with God and the enemy. I've written about these life-altering interactions in two books: *Revelation Driven Prayer* and *The Coming Church*. I've told these stories in churches around the world, but this particular story rocked me to my core.

Mission Manitou

In Manitou Springs there is a large cave system where we would often host an event called Mission Manitou. We took visiting teams into the caves and prayed in there in perfect darkness, without moving

Capturing the Supernatural: Healed!

around or leaving—for four to five hours. It was even more powerful and transforming than it sounds. People met God in the caves time and time again.

One particular week, a team of thirty young adults arrived for seven days of training, prayer, and encounter at a Mission Manitou event, but nobody realized just how significantly God was going to move.

As they disembarked from the van they rented to shuttle them from the airport to the church, they filed into Revolution House of Prayer (RHOP). My team was waiting for them. Even before we welcomed them, we began praying over them and prophesying. It was quite a first step for these new recruits!

I prayed for one young lady named Chelsea and was overwhelmed. My spirit was burning as I was contending for her in prayer. I felt tears flood my eyes as I had a revelation that Chelsea was in store for a major breakthrough. Little did I know that she had never experienced God in her life. Little did I know just what was going to take place as the week came to a close.

> I felt tears flood my eyes as I had a revelation that Chelsea was in store for a major breakthrough. Little did I know that she had never experienced God in her life.

The days were filled with prayer meetings, teaching, prayer walking, and prophetic exercises. The young men and women of God were coming alive as they allowed the Holy Spirit to pour over them, wave after wave, day after day. We were witnessing amazing miracles and their hunger was increasing. In the midst of all of this forward momentum, Chelsea remained frustrated.

Chelsea was a very sweet, soft-spoken young lady in her early twenties. There was nothing harsh or aggressive about her. As I continued to passionately pray for her to have an encounter with God, she maintained her kind disposition. She was disappointed that her meeting with Jesus was delayed, but she didn't disengage. She held out hope that a visitation would be hers. I was holding out more than hope,

Prayer in the Cave

however. I was angry. I was furious that the enemy would so brazenly assault such a hungry soul, and I was determined to annihilate him.

As the week progressed, more people were getting transformed by God, and Chelsea simply wasn't. I continued to share prophetic words to encourage her with tears in my eyes.

The last day of this Mission Manitou event was on a Sunday, and it was to be a day of impact. After a morning and then an evening service, we were scheduled to venture into the caves for the climatic conclusion of our time together.

Time was short and I was becoming increasingly agitated in my spirit. Chelsea was seemingly no closer to a breakthrough than the first day she arrived. After the evening service concluded, the group started to get their equipment together for our night together in the cave. I walked up to Chelsea and asked, "So, have you had your breakthrough?"

She said in the soft voice that I had become so accustomed to, "Not really."

I looked at her with fire in my eyes and determination in my spirit and said, "You're going to!"

I was attempting to find any way possible to encourage Chelsea. The thought of everybody else having a life-changing experience with Jesus except her was maddening! God had put her on my radar the very first day, and there was no way she was leaving without an encounter with Jesus Himself!

In the middle of all this, I heard that Chelsea was about to enter chiropractic school. Maybe she could help me. I had what I called the pinched nerve from hell in my right shoulder. Oftentimes the pain was unbearable, and it had been constant for at least eight months. It felt like someone was driving a nail through my shoulder. I had gone to a chiropractor and massage therapy with no success. I was grasping at straws regarding Chelsea, so I went up to her just before we got into the vans to head to the caves and said, "I heard you are going to chiropractic school. Maybe you have a special anointing in that area!" I told her

CAPTURING THE SUPERNATURAL: HEALED!

about my shoulder and asked if she would pray for me. She began in an extremely soft, passive yet genuine tone, "Dear Jesus, I pray for Pastor John. Would you heal his shoulder? He should not have this pain. Please heal him in Jesus' name. Amen."

She looked at me and asked, "Are you healed?"

Truthfully I answered, "Well, not really."

She looked at me with a rare boldness and said, "You're going to be."

Oh, yeah, it was on!

Prayer in the Cave

As we prepared at the entrance of the caverns, we alerted everybody that we'd be down in the earth for four to five hours—and that there are no bathrooms down there! We would be heading in at any time, and once we were down there, it would be impossible to move because of the darkness. Suddenly the lines to the restrooms were long.

Excitement was high as the sense of mystery increased for these hungry, passionate lovers of Jesus. With gear in hand, we started walking down into the cave. Once in we gave some final instructions as people found their new home on the floor for the next several hours. That particular room was about the size of a basketball court, though it wasn't a perfect rectangle. Chelsea and the others found various crevices and irregularly sized gaps to settle in to. Then, the lights went out.

That experience alone was dramatic. The darkness is perfect. Though your mind may play tricks on you with images darting about in the blackness, you literally cannot see your hand in front of your face. Suddenly you realize you are without one of your most important senses in an unfamiliar place and unable to leave. It was time to invite God into the room.

Four Seasons

When we're in the cave, we train teams in a prayer principle found in my book *Revelation Driven Prayer*. It's the one hundred percent effective prayer experiment. The concept is simple: hear God's voice as

Prayer in the Cave

He reveals His will and then believe it and decree it—and then it comes to pass. To help model this to the students of prayer in this environment, we take them through four distinct seasons or phases.

Repentance

I coached the group as we began each season. Their initial instructions were to repent publicly. There's something about being underground and in the dark that causes inhibitions to lessen. Slowly we began hearing people speak up, each in turn, and repent of sins and failures in their lives.

In the early stages we'd hear simple confessions like, "God, forgive me for my pride," or "I repent for hurting my friend." As time progressed the passion in people's voices escalated, and though it was not possible to see tears running down anybody's face, you knew they were soaking the cave floor. You could feel freedom exploding in people's lives. They repented of things they might never admit to in a regular church service. Relationships were restored as people asked for forgiveness from others. To say it's a powerful moment would be a massive understatement. Though we couldn't see our watches in the dark, it must have been at least an hour and a half before we were ready to enter into the second season.

Worship

Try to imagine that cavern full of desperate people—people who have just unloaded what felt like billions of pounds of sin and guilt into the outstretched arms of their loving Savior. We could have left right then and had dramatic testimonies of liberty to share. We could not leave, however; there was much left to be done.

Now, in that cool, dark, musty cave people were on fire and alive—some for the first time in their lives! What happened next was awe-inspiring. With no instruments or skilled singers, we entered the next phase—we worshipped.

Thirty people singing a worship song in that environment is something to hear. The echoes of glorious song from the throats of newly freed people

CAPTURING THE SUPERNATURAL: HEALED!

will change you forever. We kept singing for at least an hour as the Holy Spirit blew through us. It's often hard to move on to the next season, but it's in the next season that we move into a place of mission advance.

Revelation

As you might predict, after experiencing snot and tears and freedom in the season of repentance, and after we engaged with the Holy One in unhindered, abandoned worship, it suddenly gets very easy to hear God's voice.

At this point, we'd been in this unusual, unfamiliar setting for at least three hours—and nobody was thinking about leaving. God's glory was all around and we wanted to know what He had to say!

I coach people to share anything they feel the Lord might be saying. People, many of whom have never prophesied before, begin sharing words, Scriptures, pictures, concepts, and other prophetic data. It's truly remarkable to listen to people so easily begin to share the impressions God burns in their spirits. It takes an encounter with God to a completely different level!

From various directions in the darkness we heard people coming alive as they shared what God was saying—and then coming alive again as they heard someone else actually confirming what they had heard themselves.

The plan during this phase is to determine a general theme. What is the one primary revelation God is delivering to us as a group? When we have that, it's time to move to the next season.

This particular night I heard a lot of excellent prophetic insight, but I didn't feel that we had that slam dunk, home run type of clarity that would make it easy to complete the next and final season. Still, I could tell it was getting pretty late so I decided to transition. I announced that to everybody but was kindly interrupted.

I heard a sweet, soft voice from the opposite side of the cave, "Pastor John?"

Prayer in the Cave

I replied, "Yes?"

She said, "It's Chelsea."

"Hi, Chelsea!"

"Ummm, I have word for you."

"Okay!"

"But it isn't good."

> What Chelsea or anybody in that cave didn't know was that I had been in severe pain for the last several hours while we were in the cave.

I start wondering what she'd say next!

I said, "That's okay. What is God telling you?"

Chelsea replied, "I see a voodoo doll in somebody's hand—and the doll is you."

As she said that I felt a rush come over me. Chelsea was on to something.

She continued, "I don't know if this is literal or symbolic, but I see them with a needle in their hand and they are piercing your shoulder with it over and over again."

Yes, it was on.

What Chelsea or anybody in that cave didn't know was that I had been in severe pain for the last several hours while we were in the cave. I had not told Chelsea on the bus exactly how painful it was. I was in the worst pain I had ever been in—worse even than the previous eight months. The pinched nerve in my shoulder was so painful that I nearly had tears in my eyes. I had been pressing my shoulder into rocks in the wall in an attempt to relieve the pressure to no avail.

It was time to risk looking like a fool. It was time to declare a healing was coming.

Activation

I boldly announced to everyone, "This is the culmination of our one hundred percent effective prayer experiment." I asked, "Who believes

Capturing the Supernatural: Healed!

Chelsea heard the Lord?" People shouted their agreement. I then asked, "Who believes it's absolutely clear that God wants me delivered and healed right now?" People again agreed.

The final phase is called activation. We decree and declare what God has revealed so His plans are activated through us.

I was recalling Chelsea's simple, tender prayer for my shoulder when we were back at the church. I knew she was the one to lead this declaration.

I asked her, "Chelsea, would you be willing to pray for me?"

Very quietly but very confidently she replied simply by saying, "Yes."

What happened next will never leave my memory. We sat in perfect darkness in respectful silence as we waited for this young lady, who had never truly experienced God before, to say a prayer. She opened her mouth and a shockwave crashed into that place. The boldest, loudest, most shocking shriek exploded out of Chelsea's lungs: "Devil! Let go of Pastor John! I rebuke you in the name of Jesus Christ!"

The entire cave was filled with the roars of thirty firebrands. The seismic reaction must have been felt for miles. In the midst of the roar, as Chelsea was encountering the fire of God for the first time in her history, I was stunned.

There's Fire on My Hand!

I felt a raging fire burn over my shoulder, down my arm, and into my right hand. My right hand had been tingling and numb all night due to my ailment. This was replaced by a burning that not only brought instant, one hundred percent healing to my shoulder, but has resulted in people sensing that fire and asking me to release it into them to this very day.

As the cave continued to fill with roars of intercession, I got their attention. After testing my shoulder's range of motion and determining that I was, in fact, fully healed, I said, "My arm is burning! It's on fire! I can't see it but I can feel it all over me! I am fully, entirely, completely

Prayer in the Cave

healed!" The roar doubled in volume as we declared the victory and gave thanks to our mighty God.

That completed our cave experience, but the story doesn't end there.

Broadway

Sometime later I received an e-mail from a Broadway drama company. They were coming to the Colorado Springs area to do research for a new project. It was to be a collection of stories about social groups in the Pike's Peak region, and it would be presented on stage as a true-life docudrama.

> After testing my shoulder's range of motion and determining that I was, in fact, fully healed, I said, "My arm is burning! It's on fire! I can't see it but I can feel it all over me! I am fully, entirely, completely healed!"

We were chosen as one of the groups. The leaders and actors were not Christian, but they were truly amazing people. We wondered if they would twist words and depict us in an unfavorable light. They did not.

They started attending some of our prayer and teaching meetings as they took notes, made audio recordings, and analyzed our culture.

One particular night they came to a special event for another group that was taking part in Mission Manitou. The room was electric as people were on their faces and pacing as we prayed with white hot passion. I'm sure it was quite an experience for this unchurched group of actors, writers, and producers!

I was prophesying over several of them, praying for them and leading the night into the presence of the Lord.

I also shared with them about other experiences I had in the cave—including my healing.

After all of the interviews and analyses were complete, they put together a phenomenal stage production that featured gay and lesbian groups, political groups, church groups, and us. In fact, Revolution House of Prayer had some of the lengthiest stage time of all.

Capturing the Supernatural: Healed!

They recreated the scene in the cave when I was healed completely with Chelsea's bold prayer and the roars of victory. They also depicted the scene where we were on our faces, pacing, worshipping, and prophesying. There was an actor who played me, which was a sight to behold! He dressed like me and used my exact mannerisms. This unchurched actor, without the slightest mockery or disingenuousness, started repeating, word for word, with equal passion and intensity, what I said in that room—including my prophesies.

That production, titled *This Beautiful City*, toured from Washington D.C. to New York to Chicago to Los Angeles, mostly in front of liberal, non-Christian crowds. They all heard the prophetic words. They experienced extreme passion for Jesus. And they watched an innocent, hungry, and desperate young lady named Chelsea meet Jesus in a dark, cold cave.

John Burton has been developing and leading ministries for over twenty years and is a sought out teacher, prophetic messenger, and revivalist. John has authored ten books, has appeared on Christian television and radio, and directed one of the primary internships at the International House of Prayer (IHOP) in Kansas City. Additionally, he planted two churches, has initiated two city prayer movements, and is currently directing a prayer and revival focused ministry school called the School of Revival. John also has a web and graphic design business and is continually developing new and exciting ventures. He and his beautiful wife Amy have five children and currently live in the Branson, Missouri region. Find out more about John at www.johnburton.net.

In the Name of Jesus, Get Up!

Dr. Micheal J. Spencer

IN THE NAME OF JESUS, GET UP!
Dr. Micheal J. Spencer

Miracles!

We all love to hear about miracles, and I love to talk about the powerful Jesus whom we serve! Jesus is still in the miracle-working business, and He loves healing people in their spirits, souls, and bodies.

I was pastoring in a small community in upstate New York and was reaching many new souls. New believers are always the easiest to train in the Word. They are not all filled up with religion or bad teaching, and so are able to more easily embrace what the Bible has to say about healing.

I had just finished a series from the Word of God on healing and miracles. It made it clear that healing is part and parcel of the atoning work of Jesus on the cross. I was teaching them that you cannot separate the blood and the body. The blood always represents forgiveness, and the body always represents healing. They are part of the same covenant, so if you believe it is always God's will to save, then you have to believe it is always God's will to heal.

I began the journey with Exodus 12:5-11 where we learned about the blood of the Passover lamb and then the eating of its body. The blood saved the Hebrews from the last plague as it passed over them, and the body healed them and strengthened them for the trip to the Promised Land. In Psalm 105:37 it declares that there was not one feeble person among the tribes when they evacuated Egypt. I then explained Psalm

CAPTURING THE SUPERNATURAL: HEALED!

103:1-3, Isaiah 53:4-6, Matthew 8:17, and 1 Peter 2:24. I finished the teaching by relating the Last Supper with Jesus when He had communion with His disciples in 1 Corinthians 11:23-26, showing that you cannot separate the blood and the body of the Lord Jesus, and that healings and miracles are the bread of the children.

Get Up!

The day I preached that message there was a man who had never heard the whole gospel. In fact, I didn't even really know the guy, but the next day I received a phone call from him asking me to come and pray for his uncle who was at the threshold of death. He said that he knew Jesus would help his uncle if we went up and prayed for a miracle!

The next day I called my associate pastor and asked him to go with me to pray for this man. We really didn't know the details and had never met him before. We didn't even know if he had accepted Jesus as his personal Savior.

Pastor Gary and I jumped in my truck and headed to the neighboring town to share the love and power of Jesus. We pulled up to the house, which was a dilapidated old farmhouse with gray shingles. We crossed the street and walked up the few steps to a porch that had not seen paint in many years. We walked to the door and the porch wood creaked and cracked. I knocked. The door opened, and there was Susan. She was quite elderly, in her mid- to late-seventies. Her hair was white and her face was creased with years of living. She greeted us with a smile, but you could see the sadness in her eyes. When we walked into the front door, the living room was directly ahead. In the living room was the hospital bed that cradled the body of a tall man, now skinny and eaten up by disease. Susan explained to us that hospice had been coming in and that James had not been awake in about a month.

I was staring at his gaunt, pale face when the front door opened again. It was their daughter who decided to come over because of our visit. The whole room was just sad, not just the people, but the environment. I was getting ready to pray when the Holy Spirit told me to ask the daughter to

In the Name of Jesus, Get Up!

take Susan to town for breakfast or a coffee. The Holy Spirit reminded me that when Jesus prayed for Jairus' daughter in Mark 5:40, He put out all those who did not believe. Susan was sweet, but I did not know whether she believed or not, and I needed to pray in the Holy Spirit and pray down the power of heaven to raise this man up. Her daughter was gracious and trusting as they left the home and headed into town.

Once they left, Pastor Gary and I were free to talk and pray with no restrictions or doubt in the room.

As I looked down at James lying in the bed, I was a little grossed out. He definitely had an aroma, and there was fecal matter on the white sheets where he lay, unresponsive. I looked over and there was Pastor Gary stroking his hair—hair that had not been washed in a long time. As you may have guessed, Pastor Gary had a gift of mercy that I did not. I immediately felt the surge of the Holy Spirit go through my body. I began praying in the Spirit and could sense my faith rising. The anointing was filling the living room and the gift of faith exploded in my spirit as I said, "In the name of Jesus, get up." James sat up! No, really! James sat right up in that bed and looked into my eyes! There are no words to describe the sensation you experience when Jesus uses you as a vessel to show His love to another human being.

> Here was a man who, moments before, was semi-comatose. Now he was looking us in the eyes and receiving Jesus as his personal Lord and Savior.

James was in his right mind and very alert. We were able to lead him to Jesus right there in his bed. Here was a man who, moments before, was semi-comatose. Now he was looking us in the eyes and receiving Jesus as his personal Lord and Savior.

We heard a car pull up into the driveway, then the porch creaking, and the front door opening. James was sitting up in the hospital bed, and when Susan walked into the room, we all heard, "My sweet Susie." James called her by his pet name for her, and she began to weep. She went to the end of the bed and they began talking. It was so beautiful!

CAPTURING THE SUPERNATURAL: HEALED!

I knew it was time for us to leave, so I motioned to Pastor Gary. Then I looked at James and asked him if everything was all right, and he said, "I'm all right now. I have Jesus in my heart." The smile on my face and heart was *huge!* Pastor Gary and I walked out to the car, rejoicing in Jesus and His loving power that He could take a man from the threshold of death, raise him up, and save his soul—in just a few moments.

We got in the car and decided to go to breakfast ourselves, and then Pastor Gary did it. He reached over to shake my hand with the same hand he had been stroking James's nasty hair. I stopped him quickly, and said, "Do not touch me until you wash those hands." Like I said, I don't have that gift of mercy, but thank you Jesus for the gift of faith and the gift of miracles!

Tumor in the Womb

Another amazing testimony of God's miracle working power concerned a couple in our church. I remember one particular testimony that has stuck with me for years. Karen and Toby, a married couple in my congregation, wanted to have a baby. They had two children from Karen's prior marriage, and they were looking forward to being able to share the joy of having a child of their own. Karen suffered from some pretty severe fertility problems, and her other two children were conceived through the use of fertility medications. I challenged them to believe God in faith for something big, and I told them to write it down so they would remember it. Karen wrote down that she wanted a baby by the end of 2009. She tucked that paper away in her Bible, believing that they would have a baby by the end of the following year.

In April of 2009, Karen found out she was pregnant. They were overjoyed! That in itself was a great testimony. However, at their fifth month ultrasound, they were given some shocking news. Their baby, whom they found out was a little boy, was in the womb alongside a tumor that was 10 centimeters in width. Karen's midwives made an appointment for her to see an OB/GYN specialist to discuss what that might mean for the pregnancy, and to find out what could be done. In the meantime, Karen and Toby did a lot of praying, and they decided they were going to go to the front of the sanctuary for healing that following Sunday morning.

In the Name of Jesus, Get Up!

Sunday came, and God gave me several words of knowledge that morning. He told me He wanted to heal people of back pain, arm pain, and headaches. Karen listened as I called those people who suffered from those ailments forward, but I said nothing about people who were having difficulty with pregnancies. Still, she turned to Toby and said, "I know he didn't mention my problem, but I'm going up there and getting my healing."

Together, they approached the front. Karen told me what the midwives had told her, and I lay hands on her for healing. When I was finished, I said, "Now, go to your doctor and get a good report."

That same week, they went to the specialist for another ultrasound. The tumor was completely gone! The test showed a healthy, growing baby boy and no signs of the tumor whatsoever! The remainder of the pregnancy was perfectly normal, and Peter, who was named after a mighty man of faith in the Bible, was born on December 28, 2009. Today he is a lively five-year-old who loves Jesus with all of his heart.

Dr. Micheal Spencer is the founder and CEO of His Tabernacle Family Church in Horseheads, New York. Pastor Spencer also originated Regent Bible Institute in 2002. Dr. Spencer is a certified coach and established Empowering Pastors to help build ministers, churches, and ministries. Pastor Spencer holds a Master of Theology degree and a Doctorate of Christian Leadership with Destiny College International. Dr. Spencer has been married for twenty-four years to his beautiful wife Rhonda, and they have three children. Find out more about Dr. Spencer at www.empoweringpastors.com and www.histabernacle.com.

LED, STUMBLING, INTO THE PLAN

Terry Smith

LED, STUMBLING, INTO THE PLAN
Terry Smith

An Unexpected Voice

"I have called you to preach."

I heard it clearly. Not an audible voice, but nonetheless just as clear and distinct as if someone beside me had spoken.

I was in a healing service conducted by missionaries who had returned to the states from their different fields of service. This night, in rural Pennsylvania, on a tract of flat land bordered by a meandering river and Appalachian foothills, these time-tested men and women had one thing in common—focus. They tuned themselves to an inward sensitivity to the Holy Spirit and to releasing His power to heal the sick. You could see it in their faces, in their movements, in their eyes—they knew faith and they knew God.

It was midsummer, hot and humid, at this old-time camp meeting. I arrived late and sat in the back where most of the seats were empty. In front of me some two hundred worshipers, their voices blending and strong, sang under an open-sided, rough-hewn wooden tabernacle erected a century before. A few young mothers stood just outside the perimeter, their children running and playing in the dirt. Further out other campers were meeting in small groups, chatting, visiting, and some were heading to the commissary for snacks.

Inside, a single, broken line of seekers spread out across the brightly lit front of the tabernacle. An old organ on a raised platform graced one side and an upright piano the other. The small handful of missionaries

Capturing the Supernatural: Healed!

who had been gathered at the front separated and, stopping at each seeker, thoughtfully asked questions and then prayed. A thin and balding missionary to Southeast Asia, middle-aged and dressed in a long sleeved white shirt with dark trousers and dark shoes, laid his hands on the head of an older man standing before him. A petite woman assigned to South America, in her thirties and with mid-length brunette hair and a lightly colored dress, went to a young woman, spoke with her and touched her on the shoulder. On the small band went—carrying an invisible presence with them, speaking, touching, and praying. The Spirit of God was coming upon the seekers, untying the knots of disease and pain and, in some cases, driving out evil powers. Healing was happening. The presence of God was filling the tabernacle, changing hearts, changing bodies, changing lives.

And then He spoke to me.

"I have called you to preach."

I am a follower of Jesus. He is alive and very real to me. In the course of following Him, I have been a pastor for over twenty-five years and in some type of ministry for over forty. When Jesus called me to preach, I had been following Him perhaps four years and was busy doing whatever I could to lead others to Christ and teach them how to walk with Him. I worked at my day job to pay my bills. I lived to know Christ and spread His love.

When He spoke to me in that camp meeting, it was the first time I realized that He had actually called me to work for Him full time and that He would provide my income. A novel thought! It engulfed me. Knowing next to nothing about seeking and then doing things in God's timing, in the ensuing years I twice tried to prematurely step out in what I thought was faith, only to fall flat on an empty wallet! Yes, back to work. It would be some years before I would finally leave my job at a ceramic research facility and see the promise of God come to pass. But the call was in my heart, and it came in the middle of an atmosphere that was characterized by absolute dependence on God; it came in a healing service.

Led, Stumbling, into the Plan

At that time I did not fully realize the place that healing would have in knowing God, following Him, and releasing His presence, but in the years to come I would again and again encounter the Spirit of God patiently and methodically leading me into the truth.

First Encounters

My walk with God began a few years before this, in the early 1970s, at the tail end of the Jesus Movement. For several years the Spirit of God moved across our nation, supernaturally revealing the living Christ and His love to tens of thousands of youth and young adults. The very atmosphere in region after region was changed as spirits of darkness were pushed back and the presence of God was poured out to directly access the hearts and minds of youth. Youth and young adults who had never even considered Christ were now encountering Him, and were radically abandoning themselves to follow Him and lead others to Him. They became catalysts for His presence and power.

Before I began to follow Christ, and in the period immediately following my graduation from high school, I went through a rather short-lived, but desperate, attempt to be a good hippie. I adopted much of the hippie mindset, clothing, and lifestyle, and gave myself to writing poetry and reading the great classics in literature, Eastern religions, and existential philosophy. I had moved to Erie, Pennsylvania, a few hours away from my hometown family and roots, and I was defining my new life by some sort of self-indulgent quest to experience and be mentally and emotionally stimulated by "whatever was real and true." I told myself I was trying to know and experience truth. I could carry impressive stacks of books and would gladly argue with anyone. Add to that a little dabbling in the occult, some mind-altering drugs, and a few nasty experiences with evil spirits and you get an idea of where I was.

In the middle of my melee, a very good friend from my childhood visited me. He hitchhiked to Erie, which is on the shores of Lake Erie, and stayed with me for a week. (In those days it was rare for teenagers or even young adults to have their own cars. It was actually common and acceptable for young men to stand along the road and "thumb a ride,"

CAPTURING THE SUPERNATURAL: HEALED!

as it was called, to their destination.) God graciously timed my friend's arrival with a lake-effect winter storm that dumped a good two feet of snow on us and on everything around us. We were snowbound, and we spent much of the next week indoors—reading, painting, playing guitar, and talking.

During that week my friend, Alex, woke up every morning, aglow with smiles and joyful expressions, opened his Bible, and proceeded to read it to me. At first I just sort of sat there and looked at him, not really knowing what to do. I don't even think he asked if I cared to listen. In our absence from each other he had become one of those Jesus people. In those days they were also known as "Jesus freaks."

Alex would start out: "Terry, Jesus is real! You've got to know Him! Listen to this. Did you know He's coming back?"

"Uh, no. What?"

Then he skillfully went to Scripture after Scripture and showed me the truth of Jesus and His kingdom. It didn't take me very long to realize that I was clueless about God and the Bible. That was an eye opener. A couple of years previous to this I had concluded that Christianity, after what I thought was an intelligent examination on my part, had absolutely nothing to offer me. That sentiment came to a head when I last ventured into a local hometown church. On this occasion I got maybe two feet within the door, stopped, looked around, and then proceeded to scold the poor usher for what I thought was his shallowness, insincerity, and hypocrisy. There the gentleman stood, his hand extended with a Sunday bulletin, as I gave my assessment of him and his church. Then I just as abruptly turned around and left, feeling very good about my behavior, and very satisfied to conclude that I could safely, from here on out, discount anything to do with church.

But, here was red-headed Alex, short, round, smiling at me, and in the midst of some sort of transformation. I saw something that I didn't really understand, but it arrested me: I saw Christ *in* my friend. The contrast was ridiculously obvious: he was plugged in and I wasn't. He

Led, Stumbling, into the Plan

radiated, he overflowed, while I just sat there, insecure, proud, self-centered, and depressed.

Alex left and went home after that week, but fortunately he proved to be contagious. I couldn't get the sense of the truth of Christ out of my mind. I began to read the Bible, almost daily. When I read the Bible, it was as if I was stepping through its pages into a reality that I found nowhere else. Somewhere I had found one of those little, orange New Testaments that the Gideons hand out. The print was very small, so I had to hold it up to my face to read it. I carried it with me everywhere. Outwardly, my life changed very little, but something was soaking in, softening my core. The love of God was falling on me, drawing me in my ignorance and rebellion.

> Outwardly, my life changed very little, but something was soaking in, softening my core. The love of God was falling on me, drawing me in my ignorance and rebellion.

Alex also loved me and prayed for me. Almighty God answered his prayers. Person after person, complete strangers, literally walked up to me and point blank began to tell me about God and His love for me. I couldn't get away from them. They ranged from a sweet, young mother with little children to a compassionate Catholic priest, from a serious college student to an old, old, smiling, white-haired man.

One evening I heard a noise at my window. I went to it and some guy I had never seen before was standing there, smiling, Frisbee in hand. I opened the window.

"Hi! I'm Brandon. I just graduated from a Bible school in North Dakota, and I hitchhiked here to tell *you* about Jesus."

"What?" I replied. I was thinking, *North Dakota? That's like over a thousand miles away.*

I backed away from the window, but he threw the Frisbee at me. I threw it back to him. He stood outside the window and threw it in again, and he didn't stop talking. He had me captured. He was such a

CAPTURING THE SUPERNATURAL: HEALED!

large and imposing fellow, like a linebacker, and he basically covered the window. I was trying to process all this when the realization dawned that everything he was saying was true. Good heavens! God did send Jesus. He did come and die for my sins on the cross. He actually died for *my* sins. But now He was alive, very much alive, and was calling me to follow him. I needed to make a decision.

I was ready. I was hungry for the Jesus this guy knew. My friend Alex had planted the seed, others had watered it, and this guy was there to reap the harvest. I made that decision and opened the door to the divine Guest. By the end of the week, Brandon the evangelist had me and several others in tow; we went out into the woods east of Erie and climbed down the side of a three-hundred-foot gorge to be baptized in the clear, cold waters of a mountain-fed stream.

At the bottom of that gorge, we took off our sneakers and stood on the sand and silt that had accumulated along the stream while Brandon talked and read from his Bible. He finished up with the last words of Jesus, after he was raised from the dead and right before he ascended into heaven:

All authority has been given to Me in heaven and on earth. Go therefore and make disciples of all the nations, baptizing them in the name of the Father and of the Son and of the Holy Spirit, teaching them to observe all things that I have commanded you; and lo, I am with you always, even to the end of the age (Matthew 28:18-20 NKJV).

This was directly from the Lord. Here we were, Jesus freaks, linked to Him and obeying His commands. I waded into the water and squared off in front of Brandon. I wanted this.

"Do you believe that Jesus is the Son of God?" Brandon began the short dialogue before he immersed me.

"Yep," I replied.

"Do you believe that He died on a cross for your sins, and that God raised Him from the dead?"

Led, Stumbling, into the Plan

"Yes!"

"Do you turn from running your own life, and do you take Jesus to be your Lord, and will you follow Him?"

"YES!"

"In the name of the Father, the Son, and the Holy Spirit…"

I don't think I heard anything else. I yielded, entrusting myself to fall backward into much more than the crystal clear water. My eyes were open, and I could see everything under the water. The round, smooth rocks on the bottom. Brandon's big feet. The legs and bare feet of a few others. I was definitely experiencing something real and true.

"This is really happening, and I'm following Jesus!"

Strong arms took hold of me. Up I came, raised from the dead.

Hunger Before Manifestation

From that time on I wanted more of Jesus. I read the Bible daily, spent time alone with God, prayed with other believers, and honestly tried to act on and share everything I was learning. Yes, I became one of those guys, much like my friends, Alex and Brandon.

There was a time when I became aware that there really were such things as demons and evil spirits. I read in the Bible what Jesus said and did concerning demons, and I read books about it. About that time I was talking to an acquaintance who had been fiddling around in some occult practices—divination in particular, and had consequently had his own personal "hitchhiker" attached to him. I lead him to confess this sin to God, turn from it, and renounce it. Then, with his permission, I commanded the evil spirit to leave him. It did! Immediately! The guy knew when it left, and he was very grateful. He was also filled with the Holy Spirit and began to pray. From then on he stopped dabbling with the occult and really tightened up his walk with God.

In those early days I didn't realize it, but the Spirit of God was leading me to experience the manifest presence of the Lord. He showed

CAPTURING THE SUPERNATURAL: HEALED!

me, either through the Bible, a good book, or through another Christian, that there was something more in God that I didn't have in my own experience. That made me *really* hungry. Once I saw something new about His love or power, I had to have it. I would spend more time with Him, read everything I could about this new idea, go wherever I thought God was moving that way, and humble myself, asking Him to change me. Eventually He manifested Himself to me in that area, and I would begin to move into what I had been hungering for. He was at work in me according to His Word:

> *Blessed are those who hunger and thirst for righteousness, for they shall be filled (Matthew 5:6 NKJV).*

The Spirit of God was strategically revealing the things of Christ to me, creating a hunger within me. He was graciously leading me step by step. He is really good! As I let that hunger lead and possess me, He manifested Himself to and through me, satisfying and filling me with more of Himself. It took me a few years to realize that, by the Spirit of God, I had been unconsciously following this principle and doing what the Bible says.

Early Experiences of Healing

While I was still quite young in the Lord I read a book by an old holiness preacher who ministered in the backwoods of Kentucky in the late 1800s and early 1900s. He would go out into the woods and fast and pray until he was clear about God's leading. The Lord would either just speak to his heart or give him visions. Once he had his orders, he just simply obeyed and went to the place he was directed and said whatever God had given him to preach. On a regular basis he saw many powerful healings and miracles that brought many people to Christ. At times the Lord used him in some tiny, backwoods village to bring a move of God that would last for weeks and result in dozens coming to the Lord.

That man became my hero, and I was determined to press into what he had. There was more about healing that I didn't understand, but I knew God was leading me and I was trying to enter in. I told the Lord, "I take You as my doctor." I began to study healing, and to pray healing

Led, Stumbling, into the Plan

for myself and basically for anything else that moved. I have to say that I was somewhat frustrated with the results, but I did not give up; for a few years I only occasionally saw someone healed.

I'm being honest here. I was enrolled in God's "school of the Spirit," but I had more self-reliance in me than I realized. One of my positive experiences came when I offered to pray for an elderly woman I had met only minutes before. While praying I saw an inward picture, a mental image, of a river that was washing away debris that had accumulated in the river and along its banks. At the time I wasn't exactly sure what that meant, but, because she had told me that she was being treated for cancer, I concluded that God must have been washing something away. A few months later someone else told me that a cancerous growth on the woman's back had disappeared after I prayed for her. I had sensed life at the time we were praying, and I had seen that impression of washing and cleansing, but I was still cautious and wondering if anything was really happening. I think her healing was just as much of a surprise to me as it was to her.

> A few months later someone else told me that a cancerous growth on the woman's back had disappeared after I prayed for her. I think her healing was just as much of a surprise to me as it was to her.

Not long after that I was involved in a motorcycle accident—not life threatening, but serious enough to put me out of commission for a while. A dear young woman didn't see me coming, and, being in a hurry, decided to just slow down instead of stopping for the stop sign. She pulled out in front me and I, doing about forty miles per hour, taught her a lasting lesson: I T-boned her little Ford, effectively ramming my bike and body into her driver's door. My last thoughts were, "I don't even have time to hit the brakes."

I lay unconscious in a broken heap on the road, and from what I was told the poor lady thought I was dead and was hysterical. Slowly I began to come to consciousness; I was disoriented and not yet aware of the pain. Legs encircled me and strange faces bent over and peered at me.

Capturing the Supernatural: Healed!

Oddly enough the face of a policeman was in fact a friend of my older brother from some years before in our hometown. What was he doing here? He recognized me and was saying something to me. It was like I was watching the movie of a strange dream. I kept seeing flashes of a little Ford pulling out in front of me and then my thoughts congealed: *I was in an accident.*

Immediately I cried out, "How's my bike?"

Someone turned their head to one side and said, "Well, not too good..."

I tried to raise myself up and look in that direction. Oh, consciousness had arrived and with it, pain. I only saw one glimpse of my broken bike before I collapsed again, unable to move.

> I tried to raise myself up and look in that direction. Oh, consciousness had arrived and with it, pain. I only saw one glimpse of my broken bike before I collapsed again, unable to move.

An ambulance arrived. The workers examined me, splinted my leg, secured me on a stretcher, and loaded me into the vehicle. By this time I was no longer disoriented. As I lay there alone in my thoughts, the Lord, who had promised to never leave me, surrounded me with His presence. I was very aware of His love and care for me; it looked like a contradiction, but I didn't care. I was plugged in to the current of His love. I began to sing that old hymn "Amazing Grace." There I was splinted and bandaged, my face bloody, somewhat smashed, and missing a front tooth, and I was singing:

> Amazing grace, how sweet the sound that saved a wretch like me!
> I once was lost but now am found, was blind but now I see.
> Through many dangers, toils, and snares I have already come;
> 'Tis grace that brought me safe thus far and grace will lead me home.[2]

The ambulance workers concluded that I was delirious, but I didn't care. I figured I probably already looked about as bad as one could, so

---
2. "Amazing Grace," by Edwin Othello Excell, John Newton, and John P Rees. Public domain.

Led, Stumbling, into the Plan

what's the difference? God was with me. He was pouring His love into me, and I sang for the joy of it.

Two months before this accident I was married to a beautiful young girl who loved God as much as I did. (Yes, for you curious people, we are still married, and more in love with each other than ever.) She was in training to be a nurse, and just happened to be doing her practicum in the emergency room of the very hospital my ambulance was taking me to. When I arrived a staff person found her and related to her that I was indeed in the ER, but the extent of my injuries was not yet known.

From her training in the emergency room, she had seen her fill of motorcycle riders carried in like pieces of hamburger and was very afraid that her young husband might be in similar shape. I could easily be just barely hanging on to life in the intensive care unit, or maybe missing a limb, or even paralyzed. Praying, and trying not to let her imagination get the worst of her, she continued working. The attending ER doctor, after examining me, went to her and said something like:

"Yes, your husband has definitely been in a motorcycle accident; he's been banged up some and he's delirious. He has a simple fracture in the right tibia, some damage to the right ankle, a separated right shoulder, a fracture in the left cheek bone, a missing tooth, some minor cuts requiring stitches, some contusions and bruises."

That was it? No separated limbs? No hanging on to life by a thread? No paralysis? The relief was overwhelming. She let out a sigh and gratefully said, "Oh, thank God! I'm so glad!"

He said nothing, looked at her, and went back to the ER.

The six weeks following the accident were less than glorious. The pain was severe. I spent a week in the hospital, mostly sedated, and then was sent home with a prescription for a weaker pain medication. That didn't work. After several days I was readmitted to the hospital for another week of in-hospital pain management. Again, I was released with the weaker prescription and an uncooperative leg that felt like it was on fire.

Capturing the Supernatural: Healed!

Four weeks after the accident I had an appointment with my orthopedic doctor. I was a mess. If you've ever been in pain and sleep-deprived over an extended period of time then you have an idea of how I felt and looked as I sat in the doctor's office. An older, no-nonsense nurse came to the waiting room and instructed me to go down the hall, take the first right into an exam room, take off my pants, sit down, and wait for the doctor. My crutches and I obeyed immediately.

It's a vulnerable feeling, sitting there on a cold, vinyl-covered chair in a small clinical room, your pants down, hoping the nurse doesn't pop in with more instructions.

The doctor came. We exchanged the necessary greetings and he leaned up against a counter and read my record from a clipboard the nurse had left for him. He came over and looked at the leg. He looked at me.

"Terry, your leg is progressing fine. It will be some months before you're off the crutches, but I don't see any problems."

Problems? From his perspective, I suppose not.

"Doc, the pain is still really bad. I hardly get any sleep," I told him.

"That's just in your head," he retorted.

"What?" I couldn't believe what he was saying.

"You just want the drugs. You have to learn to handle this without them. No more pain medications."

He made a few notes on the clipboard, said nothing more, and unceremoniously walked out and went down the hall to another exam room. I was left with my pants down and my mouth open. I gathered myself together, got my crutches, and hobbled out.

Now, as a side note, I can say with all clarity that the pain was definitely in my leg. Later, I was told that because of my leg injury I had regenerating nerve pain, which could be quite severe and go on anywhere from a few months to a year.

Led, Stumbling, into the Plan

During the next two weeks I spent a lot of time moaning in pain and rolling in my bed. I had no appetite. I lost, altogether, twenty-five pounds, and I was unable to sleep. Occasionally I would pass out for a couple of hours due to exhaustion. I did what I could to read the Bible, seriously talk to God and believe, but I wasn't seeing any change in my condition.

At the end of this two-week, no pain medication time I was visited by two of my Christian friends. Bill and Cheryl drove about an hour to get to my house, and they told me they had been praying for me. They said the Lord had told them to come and pray for my healing. They prayed quietly and simply. I don't know if I could even hear them, but after a few moments the pain began to decrease, like water draining out of a sink. Draining, draining, until, for the first time in weeks, I felt peace and genuine relaxation. I think I fell asleep before they even finished praying.

> After a few moments the pain began to decrease, like water draining out of a sink. Draining, draining, until, for the first time in weeks, I felt peace.

That was it. Short and very, very sweet. My Father did that for me. He found someone who would be obedient to come and pray for me. I still had a lot of mending to do over the next ten months, but ninety to ninety-five percent of the pain was gone, and I could easily manage or even ignore the little that remained.

Learning God's Way of Faith and Healing

Within a year I was basically mended and back at work. I used the eleven months that I was laid up to seek God. The Lord taught me many things during that time that I still benefit from today. In the years to come I continued to read the Bible ravenously, but there were still areas concerning faith and the promises of God that I did not fully understand. In praying for healing, I had my own standard operating procedure: if I prayed for someone to be healed and I felt the anointing, I felt somewhat confident that God was healing the person. Without realizing it, my faith

CAPTURING THE SUPERNATURAL: HEALED!

was mostly limited to whether I felt the anointing or "saw" some type of mini-visions or not. It was not based on knowing God's heart, His revealed Word, and what Jesus accomplished on the cross.

My wife and I had been members of a house church for several years, and I was involved in weekly street evangelism. We very rarely saw anyone healed in our house church meetings, and, although I did see people occasionally come to the Lord on the streets and in our coffeehouse ministry, I never saw healing happen as an aid or stimulus to evangelism. I had, unfortunately, been influenced by the teaching in our house church as well as some accepted and traditional theology, that God in His sovereignty might choose to do other than what He seemed to be saying in the Bible. In fact, I had been taught that it was presumptuous and rebellious to expect God to heal or answer our prayers "on demand"; instead we should first seek God and see if it was His will. If He indicated that it was, we were on safe grounds for faith.

In the early days of our house church, the group had been life-giving and affirmative, but over the years the teaching and the group became dry, critical, and exclusive. Eventually we were told not to mix with believers from other groups and to stay away from current teachings on faith. The group eventually broke up. About that time God moved some believers into my town who were committed to intercession and evangelism. We began to fellowship, pray, and evangelize with them. They were strong in the Word of God and faith and were determined that I was going to read their books. My wife and I loved these other young couples, but because of my previous teaching and my own pride I resisted their attempts. I wouldn't read the books or listen to any of the teachings.

That is, until James and Sally came along. They moved to our town because James had been hired at one of the local banks. We became good friends with them, and they became a part of our circle who met together to worship, pray, teach, and encourage each other, and go out and preach to others. Sally had time on her hands and often visited us. Everywhere she went she brought her small cassette tape player with her; she listened to it almost constantly. I can still picture her happily

Led, Stumbling, into the Plan

sitting in our living room, listening to faith teachers, the very ones I had been warned about. She was never content to listen quietly; the volume was so loud that the words were inescapable. I think I involuntarily listened to many hours of such teaching. Nevertheless we developed a great friendship with James and Sally. They sincerely loved God and were great fun to be around.

Getting back to that stubbornness of mine. God loves us, has a wonderful sense of humor, and knows how to get our attention. I remember very distinctly that I was praying for our local region and was keenly aware that the Father wanted to give me some type of revelation that would enhance my ability to intercede accurately. I knew I was up against my need, and I was stretched out to God, looking to Him and waiting on Him for his answer. At one point in my praying my desire became very intense, and suddenly I began to hear one of Sally's teaching tapes giving me my answer. Only there was no Sally or cassette player anywhere near me; I was alone, praying and driving my car on a straight stretch that led out of town.

I was astonished as I listened to what this teacher was saying. I'm sure I was hearing it in my mind, but it was more than suddenly remembering and then clearly thinking about something I had heard previously. No, I was *hearing* the sound of the man's voice, not recalling or thinking about it. For the first time I heard what this teacher was saying, and it was just what I needed.

I was finally at the place where I was willing to listen, and when I heard it, I loved it. I ate a good measure of humble pie that day. I think I ate the whole thing! I had to keep eating so that the Holy Spirit could peel away layers of erroneous religious tradition that had been deeply entrenched in my thinking.

Once again the Holy Spirit was graciously and freely orchestrating my walk with Jesus, and He was presenting more of God to me. I began to see healing as the promised will of God, and that it had been provided for, along with forgiveness, in the death of Christ.

Capturing the Supernatural: Healed!

When I discovered that *every* promise in the Bible is indeed the Word of God, to be taken and acted upon at face value, I began to see God and His Word in a new light. I went from praying for healing to see what would happen and *hoping* God would act, to *knowing* that God wanted me to take hold of and release the *fact* of His healing.

My wife and I were in agreement on pursuing God. Of course, we began to read the books, devour the teachings, and base our believing on the pure Word of God in a way that we had not understood before. Because we were so hungry, we went to Philadelphia for a large several day conference on faith and healing. Perhaps 5,000 were in attendance, and the atmosphere was thick with the presence of God.

The main speaker knew the Scriptures like no man I have ever heard before. He opened the Word in a way that brought you into the power of it. He injected his teaching with stories of how he had learned God's ways, and of his experiences of His love, mercy, glory, and power. The man never knew it, but I adopted him as one of my spiritual fathers, and poured over many of his books and teachings.

One evening this man was praying for a long line of those seeking healing. As he stood before each person and prayed for them, I watched how they responded as the Holy Spirit came upon them. Some collapsed or melted to the floor. Some stood and quietly worshipped the Lord. Some began to vibrate as if they were plugged in to electricity, and one flew backward several feet as if shot by a high-powered rifle. My hunger was focused on the Lord Himself to receive the anointing to minister healing. I got out of my seat and, keeping myself about fifteen feet away from the minister, I followed him as he prayed his way down that very long lineup and ministered to each person. I *had* to have the anointing that was on him. As I followed him, my faith connected with him and the Holy Spirit, and I just soaked or absorbed the power of God that was present. I didn't have any particular feelings, sensations, or visions

Led, Stumbling, into the Plan

as I followed that man, but my heart was open wide and my faith was reaching out to take what God was offering me.

When I returned from that conference I began to see immediate results as I boldly prayed for people. I now believed that God was in it every time I prayed for someone. I still quieted myself to be led by any impressions He might give me, but I now believed that healing was definitely His will, and that He was there to perform His will and do what He had said in His Word.

Many times, when I laid hands on someone, I could tell if they were receiving or not. Sometimes I had insight on how to encourage or instruct them so they could make an adjustment in their thinking or believing. I saw that God wanted to heal each person and that, if I cooperated with Him, I would see many more people healed and impacted by the love of God.

Yes, I did realize that there would be times when, in a given situation, no one would be able to bring healing. That happened to Jesus in His own hometown. But that was the exception in His ministry, not the norm.

Over the years I have ministered in many different situations and have almost always prayed for healing whenever there was a need. I've met people and have seen God heal them in homes, coffeehouses, churches, sidewalks, outdoor fairs and festivals, hotels, and grocery stores. I'll relate the stories of a few of the many healings God has privileged me to see.

The Vacuum Cleaner

Mark had felt out of place, ignored, and even somewhat rejected at a local church, and he was searching for somewhere else to go. His wife was also hurt, even offended, and now refused to attend any church. He was under a doctor's care for three medical conditions, and when he heard about a meeting I was having in a home, he came. Perhaps a dozen people, all friends, chatted together and laughed as they sat in chairs scattered around a large living room. Mark came in right before we started and, smiling slightly, he quietly introduced himself and sat down in a corner. He was in his late twenties, tall, thin, with long, almost shoulder-length blond hair; he only briefly made eye contact when he spoke. We opened

Capturing the Supernatural: Healed!

the meeting by singing to the Lord, interspersed with spontaneous prayers and expressions of praise from those in the room. Mark remained quiet and motionless in his seat. At one point in the singing, the thought came to me that he needed physical healing and that some sort of curse was the cause of his ailment. I stopped the worship and addressed him.

"Excuse me, Mark. I believe the Lord wants to heal you, and that a curse is causing your problem."

He was startled, and said, "I didn't know if the Lord wanted to heal me or not, so I asked God to tell you if He did."

"Would you like me to break this curse for you?"

At that time I knew nothing about Mark or his background, but apparently he was connecting with my words. He looked a little apprehensive, but said, "Yes, I want you to do that."

I got out of my seat and went over to him, and said, "In the name of Jesus I break the curse that has been passed down on this man. I command the spirits associated with it to leave. Lord, come and heal all the damage that was done, and fill him with Your Spirit."

For a few moments everyone in the room was quiet. Mark was swaying slightly, his eyes closed. He took a few deep breaths, opened his eyes, and said, "Something came down over me. It felt like a vacuum came down on me and sucked everything up out of me. Everything. It went right up through my head. Then a breath came and blew into me and filled my lungs. The pain is gone!" He looked happy and dazed.

I asked, "What was your condition?"

"I've had three conditions—my thyroid levels have been off and I'm about to go on medication. I've had a painful disease of the intestines, and I've had migraines for years. The pain in my stomach is gone!"

After the Lord healed him that night Mark became a regular at the meetings and really grew spiritually and emotionally in the love of God. Further testing showed that his thyroid levels were now normal, and the migraines did not come back. However, a few weeks later he asked for prayer.

"My intestines are inflamed again; it's like they are raw." He was obviously suffering.

That sort of thing makes me mad when it happens. Diseases should not be put on people. I knew he needed instruction to activate his faith. Then, when I prayed for him, he would receive healing again, but be able to retain it.

"God has already healed you, and He didn't take that blessing away from you and put this sickness back on you. You know what His will is, so when God heals you, you have to take a firm stand against any symptoms if they return."

He just looked at me. I didn't think he was quite getting it yet, or at least he didn't know what to do with the information I was giving him. I continued: "In Luke 10:19, Jesus says, 'Behold, I give you the authority to trample on serpents and scorpions, and over all the power of the enemy, and nothing shall by any means hurt you' (NKJV). You have to run to them and trample them! You cannot allow yourself to be dismayed or caught off balance. The enemy will try to intimidate and deceive you, if he can. You have to use your authority, speak to him, and make him leave in Jesus' name! Will you do this?"

"Yes, but I don't know how. Can you help me?"

I spoke and he repeated: "Father, I know that You healed me. I know that You did not take my healing away from me. I believe this, and I know that I can resist the Devil and receive my healing back again. Satan, I am under the authority of Jesus Christ. I command you to leave me and take this disease with you."

I said the words for him, which he repeated after me. He needed to practice and learn how to use the authority Christ gave him. I could tell that he was sincere. I again prayed for him, and immediately the pain left. This time he retained his healing.

CAPTURING THE SUPERNATURAL: HEALED!

"You Are Going to Pray for Me!"

I was invited to hold meetings in Virginia. Some of the meetings were in the home of a gracious couple from El Salvador. I spoke on prayer, and although the meeting was good, it seemed to be on the quiet side. When it seemed that all was finished, the couple closed the meeting and I was about to step out of the corner from where I had been speaking when a large woman quickly approached me and stood in my way.

"Oh, no, you don't! You aren't going anywhere," she blustered out.

She was dark-skinned and wore a brightly colored dress. With her long, jet-black hair pulled back behind her ears, and her eyes determined, dark and piercing, she was practically in my face.

"Yes, ma'am!" I felt it was best to be agreeable.

"You are going to pray for me. I need healed!"

"Yes, I will. I think you know my name. I'm Terry, but I don't know yours?"

She told me her name, Maria, and went on to tell me about fibromyalgia and pain in her neck and shoulders, and a strange condition in her toes. I looked down at her feet. She wore open-toed sandals, and I could see that all of her toes were drawn back, severely bent at the joints, and dark purple.

"I'm scheduled to have them all broken, stretched out, and reset. And that's next week. Have you ever had a toe broken? I want mine healed!"

I looked at the toes. I looked at her. I knew there would be no negotiating on this one. Although her hands were no longer on her hips, she was still standing in my way and making direct eye contact, occasionally waving her hands for added emphasis. She needed a miracle. I felt we should first pray for the fibromyalgia, which didn't seem quite so imposing. This would build faith in both of us.

"Maria, let's start with your shoulders and neck. I believe we'll see healing there, and then we can go to the toes."

LED, STUMBLING, INTO THE PLAN

She closed her eyes, lifted her head, and waited. I quieted myself and checked with my spirit to sense any direction the Lord might be giving. Everything seemed good; I had a green light. I began to pray: "Lord, Maria belongs to You. Come and surround her with Your healing presence."

I waited a few moments to see what God was doing.

"Maria, is it okay if I touch your shoulder while we pray?" I gently stretched out my hand, my fingertips almost touching her. Without opening her eyes, she nodded her head and I spoke again: "Pain, I serve you notice. You cannot stay here! Fibromyalgia, I command you to leave in the name of Jesus."

I spoke to the condition as though it had a personality and I commanded it to leave her. As she had done with me, I got into the face of the thing and refused to take no for an answer. I commanded it a few times and then stopped and asked her what she was feeling.

"It's getting better! The pain is going!"

When I am praying for someone either for deliverance or healing I tend to pray with my eyes open. This allows me to keep a careful eye on the person and their needs. So with my eyes open, I prayed: "Father, we thank You for what You are doing. We believe for the complete healing. We receive what You are giving. Pain and fibromyalgia, leave in the name of Jesus, and take with you all that you have brought."

I waited a few moments, then asked her, "Maria, what's happening?"

She was smiling profusely. She opened her eyes and clapped her hands.

"Gone! All gone! No more pain! Thank You, Jesus! I love You, Jesus!"

Her joy was absolutely beautiful. She went on for a short time like this, clapping her hands like a child, praising and loving Jesus. Then she looked at me again, almost mischievous, tilted her head to one side and raised her eyebrows, as if to say, "Well, shouldn't we continue now?"

I responded, "I think it's time for your toes to rejoice. Shall we?"

Capturing the Supernatural: Healed!

"YES!"

By now both of us were enjoying the love of God and boldly expecting a miracle. I looked down at Maria's feet and spontaneously said, "Toes, in the name of Jesus I command you to straighten out."

I repeated the command a couple of times and briefly waited. She said nothing. I saw nothing and felt nothing. Again I spoke: "Toes, line up with the Word of God. All disfigurement, all discoloration, all pain, leave now!"

I continued in this vein for maybe thirty seconds. Then she squealed!

"They're straightening out! Look! Look!"

Slowly, over the next few minutes, as we thanked God and commanded in Jesus' name, her toes extended and the discoloration receded until they were completely normal and pain free. This dear, precious child of God grabbed me, held me to her bosom, bear-hugged me, and kissed me long and hard on both cheeks! I think it was a cultural thing with her, but I was afraid I was going to get it on the lips, and I was planning my escape. I wasn't sure how I was going to do that, but thank God I didn't have to do anything. She let go (I think the Lord heard my prayer), thanked God and me over and over, did a little dance, and left.

> Her toes extended and the discoloration receded until they were completely normal and pain free.

God is good! On all accounts.

The Action of Faith

The setting of this story is a small, rural church in eastern Ohio that I ministered at a couple of times a year for several years. We knew many of the people there on a first-name basis. When I ministered there on Sunday mornings I usually arrived early to pray with the pastor before the meeting began. One particular Sunday morning I was standing at the front, looking back over the seats, praying and thinking about the

Led, Stumbling, into the Plan

meeting that would soon begin, when Bill and Marsha entered the room from the back.

I knew this couple well, having eaten in their home and prayed with them many times. They were in their early thirties and very talented. Bill was a writer and Marsha, an artist. Both had come to the Lord from dysfunctional, broken families. They had found refuge and healing in the unconditional love of the Father and were always at church whenever the doors were open.

Evan, a man who looked like everyone's grandfather, was the pastor of this church, and he told me that he had originally found out about them from Bill's aunt. She occasionally visited their meetings and was often present when I was invited to minister there. Evan told me about the time Bill's Aunt Sue had called him late one Saturday evening; their conversation went something like this: "Pastor Evan, this is Sue Malechi. I want to ask you if it's okay if my nephew Bill and his wife come to your church."

Evan thought to himself, *"Had this fellow done something? Was this Bill infamous and I just didn't know about him?"*

"Why, yes, of course they can. Is everything okay with him?" he asked. Evan was a true pastor. Much of the growth in the church had come because of his love for people. Sue went on: "Well, he's big. He may not get in the door. He's born again, but he's very embarrassed about his size. He's afraid he may not get through the door and that if he does, he may not be welcome."

Relieved, Evan said, "Tell him not to worry about it. The entry doors in this place are quite wide and he will be more than welcomed; he will be loved."

Bill and Marsha showed up the next day, hungry for God; they were soon captured by the presence of the Lord and the love they found there. Many times, when I stayed at Evan's house, he and his wife told me the stories of how God had transformed the lives of people like Bill and Marsha. He had a pastor's heart for God's people.

Capturing the Supernatural: Healed!

This particular Sunday morning, when I saw Bill, it was plain that something was wrong. His face was pale and drawn; he took slow, deliberate steps. Evan was standing beside me. He leaned slightly toward me, turned his head, and quietly said, "This is the first Sunday Bill has been in church for two weeks. He had an operation and has a drainage tube in, and he's had a lot of pain in the area around the tube."

I knew Bill. I almost ran to the back to reach him. Naturally speaking, Bill should have stayed home; he was in a lot of pain and in no condition to be out. But he had forced himself to come because he knew God would meet him. I was seeing, in him, the action of faith.

Without speaking to each other, I began to address the pain and whatever was causing it: "Pain, go! In the name of Jesus, healing come."

God's provision for him was a *fact*. Because I knew the Father's heart, I was able to boldly release the reality of that healing. It was only moments until the four of us were worshipping our wonderful God. Bill had been instantly and completely freed from the pain and, under the doctor's and the Lord's supervision, his wound completely healed and he recuperated.

"I Can See!"

In the late 1980s, I was in another rural church, only this time in a town where the edge of the Blue Ridge Mountains come up into southern Pennsylvania. It was a Wednesday evening seven o'clock service and it had taken me a little over three hours to drive there. I had just barely arrived when Joanne came into the sanctuary, walked right up to the pastor, and desperately cried out, "I need prayer! It's getting worse and I can barely see!"

It was about 6:45 p.m., but it appeared that this woman was starting the meeting early. Joanne stood a few feet from the pastor, tense with emotion, and was about as desperate looking as anyone I have ever seen in all my years of ministry. She was tall and thin, an attractive woman, well dressed, and in her early forties.

Led, Stumbling, into the Plan

This was my first visit to this church, and I had been invited by the pastor to teach on what the Bible calls the gifts of the Holy Spirit, and also to offer prayer for healing. The pastor had come from a very conservative church background, and had never seen God heal or do anything supernatural. He had recently found and read some books of what God was doing in many individuals and churches, and he was hungry for more. He would read a book and then pass it around the church. By this time the whole church, some fifty members, was open and wanting God to move, but no one was sure what to do. Through a mutual acquaintance he had heard of me, contacted me, and asked me to come to his church and minister.

Here he was, on the spot with Joanne. He was speechless and obviously flustered; he looked like the life had just been drained out of him. He turned and pointed at me, and said to her, "Tell him your story! He's our speaker tonight. He'll pray for you."

She paused, turned her head, and looked at me. I smiled, introduced myself, and went on: "Your pastor asked me to come tonight, teach about the Holy Spirit, and pray for people. I think I'm in the right place and I would love to pray with you. So, what's happening?"

A few people drifted in and took seats not far from us and quietly listened. A well-dressed, intelligent looking man about Joanne's age came in, walked up to the front, and joined us.

"Oh, this is my husband, George," Joanne said as she moved slightly aside so I could shake hands with him. "He's been so encouraging to me, but I still need a miracle."

The pastor sat down in the front row, and we followed suit, also sitting down. Joanne began her story. "About the middle of last week I started to have trouble with my eyes. It seemed like I just couldn't get enough light. I'm an accountant and I have to work with numbers all day. I have to be able to read ledgers, run calculations, and prepare reports. I moved my desk right in front of a large window and added more lights, but it just kept getting worse. Sunday morning, when I came to church, I couldn't even see the faces of anyone more than thirty

CAPTURING THE SUPERNATURAL: HEALED!

feet away. A few of my friends prayed for me that morning and put me on the prayer chain."

She turned to the pastor.

"You know, Pastor, when they prayed I *felt* God's presence, and I was hoping everything was going to be okay. But it's worse now!"

She was trying not to be emotional. One of the ladies seated behind us took a tissue from her purse and offered it to Joanne. She wiped her eyes, collected herself, and turning back to me, continued, "Tuesday I went to my doctor and I couldn't read any of the letters on the vision chart. He sent me right over to the hospital where they ran tests on my eyes. The upshot is that I have lesions on both of my eyes, and there is a lot of fluid buildup. By this morning I couldn't read anything unless I went out into the bright sunlight."

She used her tissue again and George took her hand.

"I told God, 'I don't see how You can get any glory out of me going blind. Father, heal me so I can tell everyone how good You are!' Then I remembered some of the stories in those books you gave me, Pastor."

She again turned to him and smiled.

"Those stories of healing were very helpful. I especially remembered one verse from the Bible in one of those stories. I had George look it up for me before he went to work. I memorized it and I've been saying it to God all day. It's from Psalm 103:

Bless the Lord, O my soul, and forget not all His benefits: who forgives all your iniquities, who heals all your diseases (Psalm 103:2-3 NKJV).

"I must have said that to the Lord a thousand times today. More than a thousand times. I'm not giving up. I really thought I was going to be healed Sunday, but I think God was looking for real faith in me. I came here tonight to get my eyesight back."

LED, STUMBLING, INTO THE PLAN

By now some twenty people had come and settled themselves in the front. Most of these people were just quietly listening, but a few had their eyes closed and were praying. This was a small church where everyone knew everyone else. Many of these people had been praying for Joanne since Sunday morning, and none of them were anxious for things to move along and for the service to begin; they cared for Joanne and wanted to see what God would do for her.

> There was sincerity, love, and faith in the room. That's a perfect recipe for a miracle. It didn't take long.

There was sincerity, love, and faith in the room. That's a perfect recipe for a miracle. It didn't take long.

"Well, Joanne, how about we go ahead and pray?"

She was no longer crying. She seemed more settled now.

"Yes, I'm ready," she answered.

"Pastor, do you have any oil?" I asked. "I'd like to anoint her."

"Oil? Ah…I think so. I'll be right back." He had to go to the church kitchen to find some oil. He returned in a few moments with a big bottle of vegetable oil. By now Joanne, her husband, and I were standing, and the pastor set the bottle on the altar rail. I was turning in my Bible to find the verses on anointing with oil while Joanne seemed to be eyeing that big bottle. She had never been anointed before and I think she was wondering just how much oil was involved in an anointing.

"Here it is," I said, "I found the passage." I read the verse out loud:

Is anyone among you sick? Let him call for the elders of the church, and let them pray over him, anointing him with oil in the name of the Lord. And the prayer of faith will save the sick, and the Lord will raise him up. And if he has committed sins, he will be forgiven (James 5:14-15 NKJV).

Capturing the Supernatural: Healed!

"Joanne," I said. "In obedience to God's Word I'd like to put some of this oil on my fingertip and touch it to your forehead in the sign of the cross. Then we'll pray. Is that all right?"

She smiled and laughed, "I was wondering how this was going to work. Let's do it!"

Several of the people in the pews rose and stood around us. They had been reading stories of healings and miracles and they wanted to see one now. The pastor and three or four of them joined hands and prayed.

"Joanne, I anoint you in the name of Jesus Christ. I declare that this affliction on your eyes is not from God, and that it is not His will. I declare that Jesus Christ bore not only your sins but also your sicknesses on the cross. In faith I anoint you in the sign of the cross."

I tipped the bottle over just enough to wet my fingertip, and then slowly formed a cross with it on her forehead. I continued: "The oil is a symbol of the Holy Spirit. He is here now because we are acting on the Word of God. He is here to do the healing. Thank You, Father, for surrounding Joanne with Your healing presence."

I waited a moment to see if I would get any specific leading from the Lord, but all I had in me was an anger that this affliction was on one of God's daughters. I deliberately released my words in faith: "Satan, in Jesus' name, get your hands off Joanne's eyes. I command this affliction to leave her *now*! Father, thank You for healing Joanne's eyes."

I kept my eyes open to watch Joanne as I prayed. She still had hers closed, so I said, "Joanne, open your eyes and tell me what you see."

She opened her eyes and looked around.

"I can see better! It's not all the way, but it's much better!"

"Let's begin to praise God for what He's doing." I looked around at everyone as I said this, and almost every person began to verbally offer heartfelt praise and thanksgiving to God. After a few moments, I again spoke to her eyes: "Eyes, in Jesus' name, *be healed*."

LED, STUMBLING, INTO THE PLAN

We were maybe fifteen feet away from a piano and I wanted to test Joanne's vision.

"Joanne, look over to the piano, please. Read the words on the hymnal."

She had her back to the piano, so she turned around and read the exact title exclaiming, "I can see!"

She looked all around the room and read several more things. By now she and a few other ladies were crying and hugging. She hugged her husband. She hugged her pastor. She hugged me.

> She had her back to the piano, so she turned around and read the exact title exclaiming, "I can see!"

As you can imagine, we had a good meeting that night. First, God came and did His own teaching by demonstration; then, we all eventually sat down and I taught from the Scriptures, and then a few more people were healed. A good meeting indeed.

God anointed Jesus of Nazareth with the Holy Spirit and power, who went about doing good and healing all who were oppressed by the devil, for God was with him (Acts 10:38 NKJV).

Terry Smith lives in western central Pennsylvania and is the founding pastor of Jubilee Christian Center. He and his wife Connie, the beautiful nurse in the early part of this chapter, were married in 1974 and have four grown children and four grandchildren. Terry and Connie both came to the Lord and were discipled during the Jesus Movement in the late '60s and early '70s. He has been involved in starting coffeehouses, churches, and house churches, and has done extensive street and outdoor evangelism. He has taught in home meetings, seminars, retreats, ministry schools, and conferences, and travels as a minister to churches as well as ministries like Aglow International. He ministers accurately in prophecy to individuals and churches, in physical and inner healing, in deliverance, and in evangelism. Terry is ordained through D.R.E.A.M. Ministries of Glendale Springs, North Carolina. Find out more about Terry at www.JubileeChristianCenter.net.

The Simple Miracle of Healing

Stephen Lewis

THE SIMPLE MIRACLE OF HEALING
Stephen Lewis

These events happened to those around me—my children, wife, and friends. God's Word is amazing, and when you apply it to a situation in the natural realm, you will be surprised at what happens in the spiritual realm. Take the Scriptures from this section and use them whenever you have the opportunity to pray for the sick. May you glean from this testimony and step out in faith in the ministry of healing.

> *You can ask for anything in my name, and I will do it, so that the Son can bring glory to the Father. Yes, ask me for anything in my name, and I will do it! (John 14:13-14 NLT)*

> *But if you remain in me and my words remain in you, you may ask for anything you want, and it will be granted! (John 15:7 NLT)*

These Scriptures make it clear that we aren't supposed to just ask God for things, we must also be in God's Word and have Him deep in our hearts. We must be seeking Him in the strength of a love relationship with Him. God wants us to have a relationship with Him; He doesn't want to be a stranger who gives on demand.

When we pray for other Christians, we must help them with forgiveness. This is a part of healing because as Christians, we are not supposed to have any type of hatred in our heart. God's Word says in Matthew 6:14-15, *"If you forgive those who sin against you, your heavenly Father will forgive you. But if you refuse to forgive others, your*

Capturing the Supernatural: Healed!

Father will not forgive your sins" (NLT). This may not seem important at times, but harboring unforgiveness as Christians will hinder our relationship with God.

The Faith of Children

In the winter of 1999, we had a bad storm in Missouri. I decided to go out and do the "man thing" and shovel the yard. In the past, I have suffered from migraine headaches that completely ruin my day. This particular day, the sun was shining off the snow and it was so intense that it irritated my eyes. I didn't realize how bad it was at the time, but continued shoveling for almost an hour and a half. To add to the situation, I had forgotten to eat that morning. I was in for a bad day. Once I finished the yard, my wife and I decided to take a run to the store. We were having a great time when all of a sudden, I started feeling strange. As I pulled into the parking lot, I started to realize that I was seeing the warning signs of a major migraine. My wife immediately went to buy me something to eat as well as some migraine medicine. My children, Samantha, who was seven, and Andrew, age five, stayed in the car to take care of me.

As I sat in the car praying that God would take this from me, a thought came to me to have my children pray for me. The faith of a child is so amazing. Whatever they hear or read about God's Word, they believe it fully, without reservation. Just as Jesus said in Mark 10:15, "Assuredly, I say to you, whoever does not receive the kingdom of God as a little child will by no means enter it" (NLT). I knew in my heart that my children would pray for me to be healed of my migraine and that God would answer their prayers. As I listened to them pray and literally heard the faith in their precious little voices, I knew they fully believed that I was going to be healed. By the time my wife came back with the food and migraine medicine, I was completely healed! Praise God! The kids were excited to see their daddy healed because they prayed! That moment was a true testimony for them as they grew older. It's miracles like this one that affect us for us a lifetime.

The Simple Miracle of Healing

A Hole in One

My wife, Barb, had a penchant for finding holes to fall in. We have a saying in our house that if there is a hole in the ground somewhere, my wife will find it! This particular day, we were leaving the elementary school after a yearly function. It was nighttime and we were crossing the school lawn when my wife tripped in a hole and fell to the ground. We quickly ran over to help her get back up and she seemed okay at the time, but three hours later she was in tremendous pain. Her ankle was sprained and was starting to swell. She could not put any weight on it to the point where she literally crawled to the bathroom that night. My wife is a nurse. Realizing the extent of her injury, she had to call work and let them know that she would not be able to make it the next morning. She crawled in pain just to use the phone that night. As she climbed painfully back into the bed, I heard her crying. For the next hour, I tossed and turned, thinking of her and the pain she was in. That's when I realized I had to do something. I got up, grabbed my Bible, and went into the living room to pray for her healing.

I got up and sat in the living room, Bible in hand, trying to figure out where to begin. I prayed asking God to show me what to do and then proceeded to read several healing Scriptures. I read and prayed for a little over thirty minutes and then returned to our bedroom and sat on Barb's side of the bed. I gently put my hand on her foot and ankle and prayed for God to heal her in Jesus' name. I spoke to God and mentioned that she needed her ankle healed so that she could function normally. I spoke of the things that she liked to do and prayed for her health and healing. When I was finished I climbed into bed and fell asleep. The next morning, Barb woke up and walked to the bathroom like normal. When she got there, she looked down and realized that she was pain free! God had healed her during the night! She called the nursing home and told the staff to cancel her replacement because

CAPTURING THE SUPERNATURAL: HEALED!

I had prayed for her ankle and she was completely healed! Praise God! That night I learned that God's Word can come to life and is living; we just have to claim it over our circumstances.

Barb's Ankle Versus the Shoe on the Step

Once again poor Barb found herself in a predicament. Our daughter Samantha was in a rush and slipped off her shoes at the foot of the steps in our main entrance. Barb stepped down the stairs with an arm full of items and, unfortunately, connected with Samantha's shoes and down she went. We quickly ran out to help her get back inside, but she had sprained her ankle again. This time it was different than the last. We immediately took action and called on the Lord for healing. I filled a bucket with cold water, grabbed a towel, my CD player, and some anointing oil. It was time to meditate on God's Word and watch a miracle happen. I have a healing CD that I like and I put that on. The CD is in both English and in Hebrew and goes through the Bible focusing on healing verses. With the CD playing in the background, I massaged her ankle and foot and anointed it with oil. To anoint means to pour or smear, and that's what I did, I poured that all over her ankle and foot and massaged it in well while praying. I spoke over her ankle and also recited some of the miracle moments in the book of Acts.

One of my favorite Scriptures to recite is in Acts 3:1-11—Peter and John are at the gate called Beautiful. The key section of the Scripture that I emphasize is Acts 3:6: *"But Peter said, 'I don't have any silver or gold for you. But I'll give you what I have. In the name of Jesus Christ the Nazarene get up and walk!'"* They didn't mess around. They spoke into the man's situation and demanded that he rise up and walk. It was that simple, and a miracle was performed.

While the CD was playing, I was aggressively praying that Barb's ankle would be healed in the same manner. When we finished, I helped her upstairs and she laid down for a nap. Three hours later when Barb came downstairs, she was healed!

The Simple Miracle of Healing

Andrew's Knee

Boys will be boys. One particular day my son was playing leapfrog with a friend in the high school gym. As my son went to reach for his friend's back to leap over him, his friend moved out of the way, and Andrew crashed onto the gym floor. After his hands met the floor, his right knee struck the ground in such a way that he thought it had cracked. Andrew came home in pain. As I felt his knee, I noticed what felt like a chipped piece of bone floating around near the kneecap. I remember thinking, *This is not good*. Sitting on the couch in pain, Andrew read my thoughts from the look on my face. Andrew had witnessed healing miracles before in his life, so when I asked him if he wanted me to pray and ask God to heal his knee, he immediately said, "Yes." I went to my office and brought out my old leather study Bible and turned to the healing section. I anointed his knee with oil, and as I massaged it I began to read healing Scriptures to him. He had faith, as I did, and as we asked for the miraculous healing power of the Holy Spirit to come upon us, he was healed with no sign of any injury. Another answered prayer! He was very grateful for the healing he received.

Brett's Broken Thumb

A few years ago, a friend of mine named Brett who works for a medical supply company was delivering oxygen when he slipped on the ice. Brett fell forward and broke his thumb underneath the oxygen tank cart. He went to the hospital that day and the x-rays showed that it was definitely broken. He went a week with a brace on it, and during that time I felt the urging of the Holy Spirit to pray for him. I called him and told him what we needed to do and we set a date. Brett is also an amazing guitar player on our worship team at church. In my mind, as I am sure in his, he needed his thumb healed so that he could worship the Lord with his guitar.

When the day arrived, we had another friend meet with us named George who was also on the worship team. For this healing meeting, I brought with me my Bible, the healing CD I mentioned earlier, some candles and a good book that I have about healing. We went into his

CAPTURING THE SUPERNATURAL: HEALED!

basement and I laid out my plan of action. The goal was to set an atmosphere of worship and meditation on the awesome nature of God. I played the CD while I read Scriptures of Jesus' miraculous healing and others from the book of Acts. In the book I brought, the author gives advice on how to receive healing and praying as well. I read through the list of suggestions and discussed them with Brett. Time seemed to stand still as we had fellowship and meditated on God's Word.

Two hours passed quickly and then we took Brett's thumb, anointed it with oil, and massaged it while we prayed. Once again, we saturated the thumb and spoke over it until we knew in our hearts that God would heal him. We talked and worshipped God for an hour or so longer and then parted. Two hours later, Brett showed up at worship practice and when John, the worship leader, asked him what he was doing there Brett told him, "I've been healed!" while wiggling his fully restored thumb in the air! Earlier Brett had told John that his thumb was broken and he wouldn't be able to play his guitar for six weeks. The next day at church, Brett stood up and testified about his miraculous healing. We were very excited to hear the news and see how God is still working in and through us in this day and age!

> Earlier Brett had told John that his thumb was broken and he wouldn't be able to play his guitar for six weeks. The next day at church, Shawn stood up and testified about his miraculous healing.

Faith of the Youth

We have a youth group at our church called "Purpose"; it is comprised of students in grades five through seven. This amazing group of children has gifts that we have seen being developed in them by the power of the Holy Spirit. One of the sixth graders named Bethany was playing basketball with some friends when a pass caught her off guard; she was hit on the tip of her finger with the ball. The pain was so unbearable she cried and thought for sure it was broken. Her parents came and picked

The Simple Miracle of Healing

her up and took her to the hospital. The doctor checked her finger, took some x-rays, and wrapped the broken finger.

Bethany had been involved in ministry for quite a few years. Her parents are assistant pastors at our church and Bethany had also been volunteering with me at Friends Helping Friends. Because of this, she had been exposed to healing miracles before. In her heart, she was waiting to see God heal her. Almost two weeks passed and the doctor wanted to send her to Bangor, Maine which is a three-hour drive. She was sent for some extra tests to see what to do about her growth plates. She was nervous but still believing that God could heal her. Before she went to Bangor, we had a youth meeting on a Tuesday night, and I was teaching the lesson. In my notes I had planned that the youth would lay hands on those who were sick and pray for them. Bethany's father, the assistant pastor, came over to ask me about having the whole group pray for Bethany's finger. He glanced at my notes and saw that I already had planned for group prayer. We took that as a confirmation that we were being led by the Spirit to pray for Bethany that night.

Once my lesson and activities were completed, I handpicked youth who I knew would take a healing miracle seriously and I asked them to gather around Bethany. Once they were in place, her dad and I coached them on how to pray for healing for Bethany's finger. To our amazement the youth prayed so faithfully and with so much passion that tears began to flow down some of their faces. They worshipped while laying hands on her and asking God to heal her in the name of Jesus. They didn't beg; they demanded the healing to come upon her. Thirty minutes later when they finished, the atmosphere was filled with the Spirit of God. It was breathtaking.

A few days later, they went to Bangor for the appointment, and to their amazement the doctor said that Bethany's finger looked like it had never been broken or even sprained. There were no sign of injury whatsoever! It was an amazing miracle! The wonderful part was that the youth were able to be a part of it, which made their faith grow even more. God definitely showed his anointing power through them that night.

I hope that these simple encounters of Holy Spirit power working through regular people will increase your faith and cause you to step into an anointing you never knew you had. The very same power that raised Christ from the dead is alive in those who come to know Him and seek His face. You too can do great things in this world just as the early apostles and disciples did. Miracles, signs, and wonders shall follow those who follow Him.

And these signs will follow those who believe: In My name they will cast out demons; they will speak with new tongues; they will take up serpents; and if they drink anything deadly, it will by no means hurt them; they will lay hands on the sick, and they will recover (Mark 16:17-18 NKJV).

Stephen Lewis is married to his best friend, Barb, and they have two amazing children, Samantha and Andrew. He is the author of the book and study guide, *Acts, the Next Generation*. He runs a non-profit organization called Friends Helping Friends. Their mission is to give out food, mentor youth, and visit the elderly. Stephen can be contacted at slewis003@maine.rr.com.

CAPTURING THE SUPERNATURAL
Ordinary People, Extraordinary God

YOU CAN BE HEALED!

Why Are Some Healed and Others Not?

WHY ARE SOME HEALED AND OTHERS NOT?

The topic of healing is comforting to many people, yet to others it can be a source of contention. Let me explain with a few scenarios.

At breakfast this morning you are checking your social media feeds and find out that someone you know just passed away from a horrible illness, snuffing out that person's life. They may not have been perfect, but they seemed to have a close walk with the Lord. There didn't appear to be a good reason for this person to suffer the way they did before they died. Before their sickness hit, they were pretty healthy overall, exercising regularly, and had a normal diet (except for the occasional soda and ice cream like everyone else). In general, they seemed to be a really great person. They didn't have too many enemies, but served their friends out of love and compassion, just like the Lord would want them to do. Had they been alive just a few more years they would have started an orphanage overseas with their hard-earned money. Why did they have to die? Was their life cut short? Who cut it out, Satan or God? Why? Wouldn't they have made a greater impact on so many other lives had they been able to live just ten more years?

Then later that same day you discover that one of your close friends had a relative who was about to die and God spared them. You were aware of the situation, prayed a few times, but not enough that you felt it would justify bringing them back from a near death situation. Although they are a great person, they have no intention of starting an orphanage or anything as grand as that. They just want to make as much money as they can to get their family out of debt and leave something for their children when they are gone. (There is nothing wrong with

Capturing the Supernatural: Healed!

wanting to get out of debt, make money, or leave something for your loved ones when you pass on.) So why did God spare this person, who will not appear to accomplish as much for the Lord as the person who just passed away who would have done so many great things for God if they had just a few more years to live?

Have you ever wondered why some people die of sicknesses and others don't? These are normal questions that go through our minds when someone we know or hear about passes away from a sickness that has not been healed on this side of heaven.

Sometimes our sophisticated reasoning steps in and we start trying to be the judge of why it was good for this person to pass away and why God should spare someone else. We go through the steps in our heads over and over again. We rationalize what just happened and why. But no matter how much we try to figure it out, we have to conclude that God is sovereign. He is God over all situations. Wouldn't it be easier, however, if we all knew and completely understood how healing works in our lives and others when someone we care about gets a serious sickness or health problem? I mean, wouldn't this prevent all the worry about whether or not this would be the last of their time with us until we see them in heaven?

How about this scenario:

You and a loved one are walking down the street on a cold, dark winter night. Out of nowhere a car pulls up and shoots at you both. One bullet hits you in the leg and several others go buzzing by your head. Your leg starts to burn, and when you look down you see blood everywhere. After checking to make sure the rest of your body is unharmed, you discover that your loved one is lying on the ground unconscious. You quickly call the police and soon the ambulance arrives. The paramedics place you on a gurney and roll you into the ambulance and off you go to the hospital. Thankfully for you, the bullet did very little damage. The great news is that you will walk again and very soon. The only trouble is a mild infection that the doctors will be able to treat, and you will need a minor surgery to get your leg back up to par. But soon you will be on your way to the physical therapist's office for a total rehabilitation.

Why Are Some Healed and Others Not?

When the doctor is finished explaining all that you are about to go through, you inquire about your loved one. It is at that time that you receive the bad news that she did not make it. Gone in just a few seconds due to someone else's bad choices. She was hit three times—one in the lower back, one in the side near her chest close to her heart, and another through her abdomen—and was pronounced dead shortly after the ambulance carried you away. The paramedics did everything that they could, but your loved one of ten years is now gone. Their life unfairly snuffed out. To add to this disheartening news, the shots were fired by a group of hard-core criminals who just happened to see you both walking and decided that they had nothing better to do but shoot at both of you to see what would happen next. All they wanted was the thrill, in their minds, of fleeing the scene and running from the cops. The hunt for them was on. Would these heartless criminals get away with it or not? Only time would tell. Should they get caught? Absolutely! But will they?

A few months pass and you are contacted by a police offer to come down to the station for some questions and updates on the crime. As you listen to the officer go through the details of the updates on the investigation, you soon discover that two of the three criminals have been caught. The third one is still on the loose and the other two are not saying a word concerning the whereabouts of the third. When you inquire as to the reason for the shooting, the officer tells you that you were just in the wrong place at the wrong time. At this the pain and memories of your deceased loved one start to sink you into despair. You wonder why all of this had to happen. Why did she have to die like this? And why weren't you able to save her? You think back on what you could have done and you realize that you did not even have time to pray while she was on the ground after being shot. Could you have prayed? Would it have worked?

Sometimes We Feel Faithless

Sometimes questions like these are never answered in our lifetimes. If you have ever lost a loved one, you have probably asked questions like these before. At one point, our family had four deaths within the same twelve month period. In May of 2013 my wife, Cathy, had a

Capturing the Supernatural: Healed!

grandfather who passed away. In February of 2014, her grandmother passed away; then just one month later her mother passed away, her life cut short. One month after that, I tragically lost my father. Cathy's grandfather and grandmother died of old age and it was time for them to transition to heaven. Her mother, on the other hand, passed away after battling through two bouts of breast cancer. The second battle took her life in a most painful way. Like all of you would do for your loved ones, we prayed, prayed, and prayed some more while watching her wither away on her living room couch, and eventually in the hospital bed that she never left the final time she was admitted to the hospital. Just one month later my father passed away from battling his second bout of cancer as well.

I thought it was interesting that both my mother-in-law and father were diagnosed with cancer around the same time and then both went into remission around the same time. Shortly after the remission, they both were hit much harder by the same cancer that came back around again. They each battled the disease as hard as they could. Because my father lived in a different state, I did not get a chance to be there when he passed away. It was hard for me to deal with this, knowing that I would never see him again. To be honest, seeing both of these loved ones' lives cut short by cancer left me feeling angry, disappointed, powerless, and in some ways, faithless. Someone looking at this situation could say that God was not big enough to step in and heal them, yet I knew that He was bigger than sickness and disease because of other experiences that I had in my life—experiences in which He showed His awesome power.

The wonderful thing is that all four of our relatives were solid believers. The moment that they breathed their first breath in heaven their bodies were restored to perfection. In the end God won! Death lost its sting and the grave has truly been denied. I am confident that we will see them all again.

> *For we know that if the earthly tent we live in is destroyed, we have a building from God, an eternal house in heaven, not built by human hands (2 Corinthians 5:1).*

Why Are Some Healed and Others Not?

If you have lost a loved one to cancer or some sickness or tragedy, and you have lost your strength or courage to stand up and fight and believe again, I know what that is like. It is hard! Your mind, emotions, and spirit feel as though you have been through a war. These types of situations require healing for you to recover. It also demands time. If you are going through something like this while reading this book, I want to encourage you to talk this over with the Lord and also talk it over with someone you trust. Don't let the frustrations stay deep down inside. The truth is that no one knows why God chooses to heal some and not others, but whatever He does, it is good for all concerned in the end.

Keep the End in Mind

There is no such thing as an instant fix for all of life's health issues, and there is no way to cover in detail everything that the Bible speaks about in the areas of faith, healing, and miracles in one book. But there are some things I think we can touch on to help as you believe for a miracle or healing in your own life or for someone you care about. I know how it feels to do everything right and to stand in prayer, just to have the person you are believing for snatched away by death. I had to face the fact that although they are deeply missed, they are never coming back; they are now in our future and not our present. This is the deep hope that we now carry. To me this means that in the end, God wins! They won!

Where, O death is your victory? Where, O death, is your sting?
(1 Corinthians 15:55)

This is the paradigm of healing that I would like to present to you. Should you be healed? Absolutely! But will you be healed every time when you want and exactly how you want to be healed? No. And if your prayers for healing don't work out exactly how you anticipate, don't be disappointed in God or angry at Him because life did not go the way you were hoping and praying for. I don't want you to think that if you or someone you

> If your prayers for healing don't work out exactly how you anticipate, don't be disappointed in God or angry at Him because life did not go the way you were hoping and praying for.

CAPTURING THE SUPERNATURAL: HEALED!

pray for does not get healed instantly, there is something wrong with you. I have been healed many times and sometimes my healing came instantly, and other times it came later. I have also earnestly prayed for some and watched them wither away. I understand how it feels to hear someone speak their last breath in tears. Sometimes it just doesn't work out the way we were hoping.

I believe for your supernatural breakthrough in healing. In the meantime, I will stand with you in prayer as much and as long as I can in order for you to help receive the victory that you are anticipating.

The following is not an exhaustive study or teaching about the topic of healing and miracles. There are whole volumes that have been written on the topics of faith and healing by many wonderful men and women of God. The following section is designed to give some biblical foundation and balance on the topic for those who are trusting God for something special in their lives. The whole purpose of the *Capturing the Supernatural* series is to help you come closer to God and to know that you can believe God to intervene in your life and situation, just like He did in the stories you read in this book. We know that God is a miracle-working God who wants to bless and help His children!

Doctors and Surgeons Are Your Friends

I have had the privilege of traveling in many states and other countries. With this privilege came many unique conversations with other believers about their views on doctors, prayer, and healing. For instance, some ask if we should have insurance. Or does having insurance show a lack of faith in God? Some may argue if God is truly the healer than we really don't need insurance, right? I have heard many different ideas concerning doctors and insurance. I believe this issue is more of a personal conviction; I do not think there is a corporate biblical mandate here that should be placed on every Christian believer on earth. Let's take a look at Luke, the physician.

Luke the beloved physician and Demas greet you
(Colossians 4:14 NKJV).

Why Are Some Healed and Others Not?

The book of Luke records some of Jesus' most powerful moments on earth through a detailed account of Luke's own personal research and investigation. God used Luke, the doctor, for this account. Today, God uses doctors for other research designed to bring healing to people.

With this in mind, since I myself have carefully investigated everything from the beginning, I too decided to write an orderly account for you, most excellent Theophilus, so that you may know the certainty of the things you have been taught (Luke 1:3-4 NIV).

I believe that we are to pray for the sick. I also believe that if the sickness turns into something serious, we should see a doctor. For me personally, it is a good idea to have a Christian doctor, and if you cannot find one, at least look for a physician who really cares. Both things are important to me. Our current doctor is a strong believer and one of the best doctors we have ever had. He cares for his patients and for those who serve under him.

As for insurance, up until recently my family went without real insurance for almost eight years. We have had to depend on an internationally based care-and-share insurance program designed to meet our emergency needs up to a set dollar amount. This type of program has built our faith tremendously. It has taught us to pray for every situation, knowing that we were limited in our resources. We moved slowly to solve any medical problem that went past prayer and our family doctor. To be honest, it has been a little scary at times, but it has also helped develop our faith for healing. Recently we found a real health plan for our two children and I must tell you that I am relieved and loving it!

I don't think it is a good idea to deny medical benefits to someone in desperate need of them. In the same manner, under today's new medical laws, I think we also need to get second opinions and research what the doctors and medical teams are saying to us when they give a diagnosis. They are human and can make mistakes too. The book of Proverbs regularly encourages us to gain wisdom in as many areas of life as possible. God's wisdom will guide us down the many roads that we have to face.

Capturing the Supernatural: Healed!

For gaining wisdom and discipline; for understanding words of insight (Proverbs 1:2 NIV).

Doctors and surgeon teams are our friends. They have been put in place by God for the people who need them. Whether they use their gifts and abilities for God's work or not isn't for us to decide. We are not the ones held accountable for that; they are. We need godly physicians in our medical complexes and hospitals more than ever. We also need to pray for them that God will guide and direct their lives and hands in every situation that they face. If you are in the medical field and would like to share some of your stories, we would love to hear from you.

CAUSES OF
SICKNESS AND
DISEASE

CAUSES OF SICKNESS AND DISEASE

Demonic Forces

Sometimes a sickness is the result of a curse or demonic force. The word *curse* means "an invocation of harm or injury; evil pronounced or invoked upon another."[3]

There are times when someone or something places or speaks or declares evil over a person's life, and that person can be cursed. It is also possible for someone to bring a curse upon their own lives. When this happens, it can open up the door to a demonic force that can be assigned or attached to a person, family, or bloodline. I am certainly not an expert in this topic, but I have seen some key curses, or strongholds, hold back people in my bloodline for years. It wasn't until the last five years that I began to notice how real these forces of evil are, and how life-altering they can become. I have also noticed that God can reveal these curses and show you how to break them off through His strength and power. This book is not meant to cover this topic completely, and we are not experts in the areas of deliverance and breaking curses. There are many wonderful ministers and ministries who have been given a calling to understand this area and teach on it. If this topic is something you would like more information about, start with the Word of God and talking to your local pastor.

> It is also possible for someone to bring a curse upon their own lives. When this happens, it can open up the door to a demonic force that can be assigned or attached to a person, family, or bloodline.

---

3. *Webster's Collegiate Dictionary*, s.v., "curse."

Capturing the Supernatural: Healed!

Is not this the kind of fasting I have chosen: to loose the chains of injustice and untie the cords of the yoke, to set the oppressed free and break every yoke? (Isaiah 58:6)

For all who rely on the works of the law are under a curse, as it is written: "Cursed is everyone who does not continue to do everything written in the Book of the Law" (Galatians 3:10).

Christ redeemed us from the curse of the law by becoming a curse for us, for it is written: "Cursed is everyone who is hung on a pole" (Galatians 3:13).

With the tongue we praise our Lord and Father, and with it we curse human beings, who have been made in God's likeness (James 3:9).

But now you must also rid yourselves of all such things as these: anger, rage, malice, slander, and filthy language from your lips (Colossians 3:8).

Why does Paul tell us to get rid of the things above? Some of these bad choices can open the door to evil being able to enter our lives and others. Consider the person who allows uncontrolled anger in their lives. They are driving along the highway when they get cut off. Already a ticking time bomb, they get so angry that they snap and chase down the other car, force them off the road, and attack the other driver. Road rage. It happens all the time today, and it is a byproduct of unconfessed sin, sin that the person will not deal with. Little footholds can turn into big strongholds if we don't deal with them. These strongholds can wreak havoc on our health and lives.

Through the years I have met many Christians who have witnessed the power of God's healing touch through casting out demons. I have seen it too in dealing with prayer ministry. For some Christians it is a normal part of their daily lives to cast out demons. I believe that this is a calling within itself and not to be engaged in unless led by the leading of the Lord.

CAUSES OF SICKNESS AND DISEASE

In Mark 9, a young boy is brought to Jesus who has an evil spirit afflicting him. At the moment Jesus meets the boy, the evil spirit forces the boy into a convulsion. This is an example of how a form of sickness manifests as a result of demonic possession or oppression. In this case, it was a convulsion.

So they brought him. When the spirit saw Jesus, it immediately threw the boy into a convulsion. He fell to the ground and rolled around, foaming at the mouth (Mark 9:20).

The disciples attempted to deliver the young boy from this demon and they could not. After Jesus delivered the boy and the main crowds left, Jesus' disciples asked Him why they could not cast the demon out and Jesus answered:

He (Jesus) replied, "This kind can come out only by prayer" (Mark 9:29).

There are demonic forces that influence people you and I meet. I don't believe that every sickness is caused by demonic activity, but the Bible clearly shows that some illnesses are caused by demonic forces. Obviously, sicknesses are not a blessing from God. They are part of Satan's attempt to stop people from reaching their destinies. It is the enemy, Satan, who comes to bring harm to everyone on earth. The battle we face in finding health and healing is truly against Satan.

The thief comes only to steal and kill and destroy; I have come that they may have life, and have it to the full (John 10:10).

Whatever you do, whatever you have to do to get your healing, remember who you are fighting. You are fighting the Devil. He wants to see as many people sick as he can for as long as possible. Sometimes people mistakenly blame God; He wants us healed more than we often realize. He is working with and for you. God is for us and not against us.

Sometimes Your Ailment Is All Natural (Too Natural!)

At my father's funeral I weighed about 241 pounds. This was the heaviest I had ever been in my life, and a large portion of the added

CAPTURING THE SUPERNATURAL: HEALED!

weight was right in my gut. The core of my body was completely out of whack. I had to watch how I got up from sitting or lying down; I also had to be careful when I exercised. I was eating healthy foods and lean meats like chicken and turkey. I drank nearly the full amount of water required for my weight; I exercised three times a week and even worked in the yard and on a construction crew during the day. So why was I gaining so much weight? There were a few reasons that I would like to share.

For one, I was eating two and three large portions at dinner each night. Not one chicken breast, but two and three. I was very hungry from all of the physical work I was doing, so I justified the extra portions. During this time I was also eating a donut (or two or three) with the construction guys for breakfast almost every day on the job site. At lunch we took turns buying each other's food at various high-calorie fast food joints. Every meal was chock full of bread and carbohydrates. This wasn't shrinking my gut any! If that wasn't bad enough, at home I would grab a scoop of peanut butter here and there and also eat a late night snack around ten o'clock.

I wasn't actually eating a bunch of chips, candy bars, or drinking lots of soda. But carbohydrates dominated my bloodstream, and that is how the weight came on so fast. About this time I realized that my waist had become a dreaded 40 inches. I decided that my life had to change.

One of the first things I did was cut out the donuts. Next, I cut out bread. I cut back on portion sizes at meals and started exercising about four times a week. It was hard, but the weight started dropping. After several months, many temptations, and unexpected turns in my diet, I am back down to 210 pounds. As a result my back feels much better, I sleep better, my joints hurt less, my energy has spiked, and my attitude has changed greatly. This was a natural healing through a natural process. I believe that there are many people, possibly even reading this right now, who have particular ailments because of their lifestyle and eating habits. Some sicknesses are not because of a curse or demon or heredity; some are just simply because of the way we choose to live.

If you find honey, eat just enough—too much of it, and you will vomit (Proverbs 25:16).

Causes of Sickness and Disease

Honey is sweet and excellent for your body, but if you eat too much you will eventually get sick. This can apply to just about any food. If we put too much of anything into our bodies (sugar, processed foods, or other chemicals), we can eventually get sick. This is why it is so important to drink a lot of water and get plenty of rest and exercise; this flushes out the toxins in our bodies. Sometimes healing is a matter of changing our lifestyle rather than praying for God to do something. I think God finds great pleasure in watching His children overcome bad habits; it brings the glory to Him as we lean on Him and learn to overcome.

Illnesses Can Be a Mix of Spiritual and Natural Causes

Sometimes a sickness is not from something purely natural or purely spiritual, but both. Let's consider an anxious person who experiences a tragedy in their lives. Now we have a nervous person who is struggling to process a bad experience as well. If they don't get their natural tendency toward anxiety under control, it could eventually turn into some type of physical manifestation. For example, someone who is nervous all the time and also required to sit for long periods of time might find themselves biting their nails a lot. Or they may discover that after a certain time sitting in the chair, they start snacking on junk food. Or their anxiety could show up as a stomach problem. Some might decide to shy away from certain circumstances that God is trying to use to bring a blessing to them because they no longer want to go out into large groups of people. Because they did not go where God wanted them to go, they miss what God was getting ready to do next in their lives. The enemy is not God, it is Satan, and he will do anything he can to attempt to keep us from God's blessing and plan. Some people grow up in poverty or extremely bad circumstances, and all they know is the way they were taught. Bad habits, unfortunately, often take a toll later in our lives. If one is steeped in bad habits and choices for too long they will eventually reap the consequences.

Capturing the Supernatural: Healed!

I was once in an emergency room when my daughter was injured. There was a thin curtain partitioning our cubicle from the next, so you could hear every conversation in that room whether you wanted to or not. Next to us was an eighteen-year-old girl who kept complaining about migraines that were bad enough to put her in the emergency room a couple of times a month. As the doctor asked certain questions and I heard her answers, it became very obvious to me that the headaches were probably due to the sin in her life more than any other reason.

Her conversation with the doctor revealed that she was on high-powered pregnancy injections to block a pregnancy from occurring during intercourse. She was not married and her mother was allowing the daughter and boyfriend to stay in the same house together. I saw a spiraling downhill cycle right there.

This family was obviously not putting their time and resources into the right areas in life. Her headaches came, according to her, when she started the pregnancy preventative shots. She had been treated several times for them to no avail. According to her, the new medications were not helping at all. On top of this, she wasn't drinking enough fluids and stayed up until three or four in the morning regularly. It is amazing how late you can stay up when you are not working. Unfortunately in our society, there are so many benefits out there for those who just don't want to work that they are not motivated to even look for work. I know this does not apply to everyone. Some people have lost their jobs, can't find work, or have been injured and can't work. I am not referring to people in those situations. I am referring to those who are too lazy to work and who have been taught how to "milk the system" just as their parents did. This kind of behavior is a generational curse and it must be broken. I was listening to the effects of this curse right next to me in the emergency room.

The wise woman builds her house, but with her own hands the foolish one tears hers down (Proverbs 14:1).

To add to the dilemma, without informing her primary care physician the young girl decided to immediately drop the shots but continue to take the headache pills while still getting very little sleep and only drinking small amounts of water. This is what put her back into the hospital.

Causes of Sickness and Disease

This young woman was not only living in a sinful sexual relationship outside of marriage, she was also not taking care of her physical body, and it appeared that her body was reacting to the medicine by giving her a severe migraine. Sexual relationships are a key element to allowing Satan entrance in the lives of people. A sexual union creates a strong soul-mate bond. It is like putting a bandage on one person, then pulling it off and putting it on another person, then another, then another; before long the bandage is so dirty that it no longer sticks to anything. This is what happens when someone passes their body around to other individuals without being committed to one person in a God-designed heterosexual relationship in a marriage covenant. Satan sees an open door and he walks right through it into their life.

Flee from sexual immorality. All other sins a person commits are outside the body, but whoever sins sexually, sins against their own body (1 Corinthians 6:18).

When you have a situation like this you are more than likely dealing with strongholds from previous practices and bad generational habits of the parents being passed down to the new generation (the daughter). She is doing what she was taught. She is only a product of what she was raised to be, unless she allows God to change her life. He can snap the chains right off. In this case, you are not only dealing with natural causes of sickness (little sleep, bad eating and drinking habits), but also with demonic forces that are either oppressing this individual or possessing one or both of the two unclean soul-mates as they engage in sexual activity outside of marriage. All this can be cleansed by the power of God's love.

So if the Son sets you free, you will be free indeed (John 8:36).

They will pick up snakes with their hands; and when they drink deadly poison, it will not hurt them at all; they will place their hands on sick people, and they will get well (Mark 16:18).

Can Healing Happen Gradually?

There are mixed thoughts and ideas about whether or not healing can happen gradually. Some people believe that healing must come

CAPTURING THE SUPERNATURAL: HEALED!

immediately or something is wrong with someone. Other church leaders teach that it does not matter how long it takes for the healing, we are to press on and keep fighting in prayer until the healing occurs. I am in the company of both groups, and so I am going to attempt to bring a balance to this controversy.

I believe healing can and does happen today and that it doesn't happen quickly enough in many of our lives. Our culture places an emphasis on almost everything other than God's ability. I don't believe people should stop taking their medication or stop going to the doctor. I do, however, believe that as the church we must get back to more powerful healing avenues for the glory of God. When Jesus healed someone, they were healed. Period!

> *Then Jesus said to the centurion, "Go! Let it be done just as you believed it would." And his servant was healed at that moment (Matthew 8:13).*

> *Jesus turned and saw her. "Take heart, daughter," he said, "your faith has healed you." And the woman was healed at that moment (Matthew 9:22).*

On the other hand, the Lord's disciples had a few unfortunate situations when it came to healing. See the following Scriptures for further study: Matthew 8:26; 14:31; 17:16-18; Mark 9:28-29.

Can healing come through a delayed process?

The answer is yes.

My brother had epilepsy for several years when he was younger. One day when he was fifteen years old, my brother came home from his EEG testing with a big smile on his face. He took the bottle of pills he had been taking, dumped them into the trash, and told me he was healed; the doctor said he didn't have to take the pills anymore. Again, I don't ever condone just emptying out the bottle of pills that your doctor prescribed for you to take unless your doctor gives you permission. My pastor teaches that if you believe you have been healed, get an appointment to see a doctor and have it verified before you do anything

Causes of Sickness and Disease

else. Then it will be documented that you are indeed healed. Back to my brother—he was told by the doctor that he would never again have to deal with taking pills in order to prevent seizures. At that time, neither my brother nor I were Christians. He took those pills for several years and suddenly came home completely fine. He has never had a seizure since. This was a gradual healing. It is also one in which God used doctors to confirm the change. The really great thing about this is that today, many years later, my brother, his kids, and their kids are epilepsy free. This is the power of God working through multiple generations.

> Miracles are instant. Healing can be instant or progressive. Both demand faith!

Miracles are instant. Healing can be instant or progressive. Both demand faith! Sometimes the miracle comes, but the person's faith is weak. Other times faith is lacking and the person praying for the healing miracle is full of doubt. Faith is required for miracles.

Truly I tell you, if anyone says to this mountain, "Go, throw yourself into the sea," and does not doubt in their heart but believes that what they say will happen, it will be done for them (Mark 11:23).

Jesus Prayed Twice

They came to Bethsaida, and some people brought a blind man and begged Jesus to touch him. He took the blind man by the hand and led him outside the village. When he had spit on the man's eyes and put his hands on him, Jesus asked, "Do you see anything?"

He looked up and said, "I see people; they look like trees walking around."

Once more Jesus put his hands on the man's eyes. Then his eyes were opened, his sight was restored, and he saw everything clearly. Jesus sent him home, saying, "Don't even go into the village" (Mark 8:22-26).

CAPTURING THE SUPERNATURAL: HEALED!

Some suggest that a prayer should only be offered once and after that never again. If you are prayed for and healed, that is great. If not, continue to seek the Lord's healing until it comes. One very powerful tool that is often overlooked in healing is speaking God's Word for the healing. This is taking God's Scripture right at His word and, by faith, speaking the Word of God over the healing need or situation.

The Power of God's Spoken Word

He sent out his word and healed them; he rescued them from the grave (Psalm 107:20).

But he was pierced for our transgressions, he was crushed for our iniquities; the punishment that brought us peace was on him, and by his wounds we are healed (Isaiah 53:5).

Heal me, Lord, and I will be healed; save me and I will be saved, for you are the one I praise (Jeremiah 17:14).

News about him spread all over Syria, and people brought to him all who were ill with various diseases, those suffering severe pain, the demon-possessed, those having seizures, and the paralyzed; and he healed them (Matthew 4:24).

By faith in the name of Jesus, this man whom you see and know was made strong. It is Jesus' name and the faith that comes through him that has completely healed him, as you can all see (Acts 3:16).

"Make level paths for your feet," so that the lame may not be disabled, but rather healed (Hebrews 12:13).

The Timing of God

There is a big difference in believing and confessing God's Word for healing and attempting to force something out of God's timing. Let's take a look at Lazarus.

Causes of Sickness and Disease

Now a man named Lazarus was sick. He was from Bethany, the village of Mary and her sister Martha. (This Mary, whose brother Lazarus now lay sick, was the same one who poured perfume on the Lord and wiped his feet with her hair.) So the sisters sent word to Jesus, "Lord, the one you love is sick."

When he heard this, Jesus said, "This sickness will not end in death. No, it is for God's glory so that God's Son may be glorified through it." Now Jesus loved Martha and her sister and Lazarus. So when he heard that Lazarus was sick, he stayed where he was two more days, and then he said to his disciples, "Let us go back to Judea" (John 11:1-7).

Lazarus had to be dead for more than three days before Jesus could raise him from the dead. Historically, the Jews believed that after three days in a tomb, the person was indeed dead. Had the resurrection come earlier, it would have not been as powerful. Someone would have wondered if perhaps it was not truly a miracle, that Lazarus had not really been dead at all. So Jesus waited. Sometimes God sets things up in order that only His Son, Jesus, will receive all of the credit for the work.

On his arrival, Jesus found that Lazarus had already been in the tomb for four days. Now Bethany was less than two miles from Jerusalem, and many Jews had come to Martha and Mary to comfort them in the loss of their brother. When Martha heard that Jesus was coming, she went out to meet him, but Mary stayed at home. "Lord," Martha said to Jesus, "if you had been here, my brother would not have died. But I know that even now God will give you whatever you ask." Jesus said to her, "Your brother will rise again." Martha answered, "I know he will rise again in the resurrection at the last day." Jesus said to her, "I am the resurrection and the life. The one who believes in me will live, even though they die; and whoever lives by believing in me will never die. Do you believe this?" "Yes, Lord," she replied, "I believe that you are the Messiah, the Son of God, who is to come into the world" (John 11:17-27).

CAPTURING THE SUPERNATURAL: HEALED!

Jesus deliberately showed up after Lazarus was officially dead and "stinking" in order to raise him from the dead, thus illustrating that God had come in the flesh as Jesus, the Resurrection and the Life!

When he had said this, Jesus called in a loud voice, "Lazarus, come out!" The dead man came out, his hands and feet wrapped with strips of linen, and a cloth around his face. Jesus said to them, "Take off the grave clothes and let him go" (John 11:43-44).

Sometimes the timing of its occurrence is important, so having discernment is crucial.

He listened to Paul as he was speaking. Paul looked directly at him, saw that he had faith to be healed (Acts 14:9).

Paul discerned that it was time for the person to be healed. Did a neon sign flash over this sick man's head telling Paul it was time for a healing today? Did the word *faith* shine over the sick man's head or flash in the eyes of Paul, signaling that it was time for Paul to pray for the man who now had faith? No. Nothing like that. The Spirit brought an inner witness to Paul that the man who was before him had an ever-increasing miracle faith growing within him, and at that moment Paul stepped into the miraculous and the healing occurred. Faith, discernment, timing, and obedience were all activated, and as a result the healing occurred.

Remember the Stones

Remember the Stones

When we sit down and talk to people, it doesn't take long before they begin to tell us stories of amazing, miraculous things that happened to them in the past—a healing, an angelic visitation, or some other divine moment that they cherish in their memory. Many times when we ask if they have ever written it down or somehow passed it on to their children, they say that they haven't. Some people go to their grave with memories of wonderful things God has done without ever passing them on to bring hope to the generations to follow. This is a sad thing indeed.

When Israel had finally crossed over into their Promised Land, God told them to build a monument of stone to remember the miracle that just took place. This would be a reminder to their future generations of God's mighty hand and provision in the hardest times they had ever faced in life.

When the whole nation had finished crossing the Jordan, the Lord said to Joshua, "Choose twelve men from among the people, one from each tribe, and tell them to take up twelve stones from the middle of the Jordan, from right where the priests are standing, and carry them over with you and put them down at the place where you stay tonight." So Joshua called together the twelve men he had appointed from the Israelites, one from each tribe, and said to them, "Go over before the ark of the Lord your God into the middle of the Jordan. Each of you is to take up a stone on his shoulder, according to the number of the tribes of the Israelites, to serve as a sign among you. In the future, when your children ask you, 'What do these stones mean?' tell them that the flow of the Jordan was cut off before the ark of the covenant of the Lord. When it crossed the Jordan, the waters of the Jordan were cut off. These stones are to be a memorial to the people of Israel forever" (Joshua 4:1-7).

Capturing the Supernatural: Healed!

> If you don't document your stories, it is possible that the life you lived could eventually be forgotten by the next generation.

Too often, when a miracle happens in our everyday lives, whether great or small, we don't make a proper memorial or way to remember what God did. We may rejoice for a while and tell our family and friends it happened, but then life moves on and we forget. What a tragedy! These are the stories that need to be passed on to create a godly legacy in our families. If you don't document your stories, it is possible that the life you lived could eventually be forgotten by the next generation.

I believe that this is one reason why all of the miracles that Jesus did while He was on earth were not written down—we are now the walking miracles who are filling the earth. We are the ones who are supposed to document and carry on the miracle-working power of Jesus Christ. You can do that by documenting and sharing all that He has done. When this happens it will build faith and hope in the hearts of the people hearing your story.

I once talked to a family that had a very unique and wonderful way of making sure they remembered everything God had done in their lives. They had a chest, much like an old treasure chest or steamer trunk, that they filled with little mementos that served to remind them of the miracles and other good things God had done for them. For instance, one of their family members had been in a bad motorcycle accident and lived to tell about it. What a miracle! They bought a little toy motorcycle and typed up the story of what happened, attaching it to the motorcycle before putting it in the chest. Every time God did something, small or great, a new trinket with a story was added. Every year at Christmas, it was a tradition in this family to gather together, open the chest, and read through every miracle, remembering anew each of the wonderful things God had done for them. It was a highlight that they looked forward to each year.

Maybe you can't do that, but I encourage you to take time and write down what God has done for you and your family. Find a way to pass along your own miracle stories to the generations to come.

How to Receive Your Healing

How to Receive Your Healing

There are many methods shown in the Bible that can be applied to praying for healing and receiving an answer from the Lord. Below are just a few.

1. Repent.

   Then Hezekiah repented of the pride of his heart, as did the people of Jerusalem; therefore the Lord's wrath did not come on them during the days of Hezekiah (2 Chronicles 32:26).

   When Jesus saw their faith, he said, "Friend, your sins are forgiven" (Luke 5:20).

   Then Jesus said to her, "Your sins are forgiven" (Luke 7:48).

2. Speak God's Word.

   For the word of God is alive and active. Sharper than any double-edged sword, it penetrates even to dividing soul and spirit, joints and marrow; it judges the thoughts and attitudes of the heart (Hebrews 4:12).

   In this way the word of the Lord spread widely and grew in power (Acts 19:20).

3. Ask for prayer.

   Is anyone among you sick? Let them call the elders of the church to pray over them and anoint them with oil in the name of the Lord. And the prayer offered in faith will make the sick person

Capturing the Supernatural: Healed!

well; the Lord will raise them up. If they have sinned, they will be forgiven (James 5:14-15).

4. Get connected to those who have faith for healing.

To another faith by the same Spirit, to another gifts of healing by that one Spirit, to another miraculous powers, to another prophecy, to another distinguishing between spirits, to another speaking in different kinds of tongues, and to still another the interpretation of tongues. All these are the work of one and the same Spirit, and he distributes them to each one, just as he determines (1 Corinthians 12:9-11).

5. Practice solitude with God. (See also the story of the persistent widow in Luke 18:1-8.)

The Lord looks down from heaven on all mankind to see if there are any who understand, any who seek God (Psalm 14:2).

The lions may grow weak and hungry, but those who seek the Lord lack no good thing (Psalm 34:10).

But seek first his kingdom and his righteousness, and all these things will be given to you as well (Matthew 6:33).

6. Always share your testimony with others. It will activate and build their faith.

They triumphed over him by the blood of the Lamb and by the word of their testimony; they did not love their lives so much as to shrink from death (Revelation 12:11).

When he arrived and saw what the grace of God had done, he was glad and encouraged them all to remain true to the Lord with all their hearts (Acts 11:23).

Therefore, brothers and sisters, in all our distress and persecution we were encouraged about you because of your faith (1 Thessalonians 3:7).

CONCLUSION

Our desire is that, through the *Capturing the Supernatural* series, people find the hope that they desperately need to see miracles happen in their lives. What you have just read is a documented account of what God is doing on the earth concerning His healing power. Through this, we believe that we will continue to fill the world with pages of the great and mighty deeds that the Lord continues to work for His glory on the earth. God is a miracle-working God. He is more than able and more than willing to work miracles in our lives. We must realize how strong His desire is to bless us in this way.

He is not a distant God who created us and then walked away. No way! He is a personal God who put His face near our face and breathed the breath of life into us at creation. Most translations say that He breathed into man's nostrils. A few translations point out that the main point of this Scripture is the fact that this was a personal touch from the Father to His children in that He came near to us and then breathed life into us. Some translations suggest that He put His face to ours, almost like a kiss, and then breathed the breath of life into us. Thus man was created. However He did it, it was personal. In a sense, He kissed us with the breath of life, and here we are.

Then the Lord God formed man from the dust of the ground and breathed into his nostrils the breath or spirit of life, and man became a living being (Genesis 2:7 AMP).

This is how personal God truly is. He wants to be a part of every aspect of our lives. He wants us to love Him more than anything else in this life. In the meantime, the Lord wants to fill the memories of the pages of our lives with great and mighty works that only He could do.

When you receive your healing, let us know! Please e-mail us at story@5foldmedia.com.

CAPTURING THE SUPERNATURAL
Ordinary People, Extraordinary God

GOD ENCOUNTERS
Life-changing Events
Coming Fall/Winter 2015

5 Fold Media is unveiling a series of books that documents God's supernatural ability working through ordinary people. For more information or to make a purchase, visit www.5foldmedia.com.

If you or someone you know has a story or video about something amazing that God has done in your life, or in the life of someone you know, and you would like to share it with us for consideration to be included in a future book, please contact us at story@5foldmedia.com

What kind of stories are we looking for? Discover more at www.5foldmedia.com.

"Jesus also did many other things. If they were all written down, I suppose the whole world could not contain the books that would be written" (John 21:25 NLT).

Want Your Church or Group to Have a *Capturing the Supernatural* Service?

Andy and Cathy Sanders have been studying and reporting on God's divine intervention in the lives of ordinary people for years. The Sanders traveled full time out of New York from 2006 to 2010; they have been in twenty-seven states and ten foreign countries. In 2009 they founded 5 Fold Media and within the first five years of the company they had produced over a hundred books. One project they worked on has sold over 300,000 copies.

In September 2013 God directed the Sanders to shift the focus of 5 Fold Media to producing a documentary that would bring hope to this generation. This *Capturing the Supernatural* series of books is being published to document what God is doing on the earth, providing a snapshot of His handiwork and incredible creative care for His children. Andy and Cathy have set out to share God's supernatural stories to America. Their ministry to the church brings an increase of faith, hope, and a renewed belief in the God who works miracles today.

To schedule the Sanders to come to your church or venue contact andy@5foldmedia.com.

Does the vision for your church, business, or organization include owning a publishing company?

God placed it on Andy's heart to pass the baton in publishing, placing an emphasis more on training future publishing teams rather than just publishing an author's book. To do this, 5 Fold Media started a publishing consulting program for businesses, churches, and companies with the intent of helping them set up their own internal publishing house. From the onset of 5 Fold Media's existence, the Sanders have known that there are more books being written and created than the mainstream publishing companies can handle. Our publishing consulting team will help your team understand and successfully navigate through internal publishing operations, external operations, staff development, international trade standard publishing, distribution, and marketing.

Because we understand what it takes to develop a successful publishing company that started without any financial backing, we will walk your team through some of the life lessons, pitfalls, and strategies that we have discovered in developing a strong press. Wisdom is attained through experience. Because of our experience in the industry we can help you create your publishing house the right way from the very start.

For more information contact Andy by phone at 315.706.8888 or e-mail build@5foldmedia.com.

Find out more at www.5foldmedia.net.

Products from the *Wisdom in Writing* series

15 Blunders
Common Errors Writers Often Make

So you want to be a writer—you've written a book, or you're just starting to get your ideas down. But in the back of your mind, you know the time is coming—that dreaded moment when an editor first reads your work, wielding their red pen of doom. Will your book hold up under scrutiny? Will you lose all hope and give up if your manuscript ends up riddled with corrections? Is it even worth it to go on from here, faced with this inevitable and mysterious trial?

What if you knew in advance what your editor was going to be looking for? What if you had a "cheat sheet" for the exam they'll be putting your book through? What if you could get your pointers straight from an editor and polish your manuscript in advance?

In this book, Ellen King gives you that "cheat sheet"—a 15-item list of things to watch out for, work on, and clean up. Having edited countless books—the brain children of authors just like you—she gives you 15 pointers representing the most common pitfalls you might be making without realizing it. With clear explanations and examples, Ellen shows you the mistakes she has seen, explains why they create problems for your book, and then offers examples of other ways to get your ideas across. Her solutions show you the best possible way to effectively connect with your readers.

For more information about the *Wisdom in Writing* series visit wisdominwriting.com

5FOLDMEDiA

We are a Spirit-led media company dedicated to:

Documenting God's supernatural ability on the earth and devoting our lives to understanding the international trade standard publishing industry in order to cultivate wisdom in writing.

Discover more at www.5FoldMedia.com.